Fundamentals of Air Pollution

BSN Raju

Oxford & IBH Publishing Co. Pvt. Ltd.
New Delhi
(*A Unit of* CBS Publishers & Distributors Pvt Ltd)

CBS Publishers & Distributors Pvt Ltd

New Delhi • Bengaluru • Chennai • Kochi • Kolkata • Mumbai
Hyderabad • Jharkhand • Nagpur • Patna • Pune • Uttarakhand

Reprint: 2005, 2018

ISBN-13: 978-81-204-1107-4
ISBN-10: 81-204-1107-2

OXFORD & IBH
New Delhi
(A Unit of CBS Publishers & Distributors Pvt Ltd)

CBS Publishers & Distributors Pvt Ltd
204 FIE, Patparganj Industrial Area, Delhi 110 092
E-mail: delhi@cbspd.com, cbspubs@airtelmail.in
Ph: 4934 4934 Fax: 4934 4935 Website: www.cbspd.com
e-mail: publishing@cbspd.com; publicity@cbspd.com

Branches

- **Bengaluru:** Seema House 2975, 17th Cross, K.R. Road, Banasankari 2nd Stage, Bengaluru 560 070, Karnataka
  Ph: +91-80-26771678/79 Fax: +91-80-26771680 e-mail: bangalore@cbspd.com
- **Chennai:** No. 7, Subbaraya Street, Shenoy Nagar, Chennai 600 030, Tamil Nadu
  Ph: +91-44-26680620, 26681266 Fax: +91-44-42032115 e-mail: chennai@cbspd.com
- **Kochi:** Ashana House, 39/1904, AM Thomas Road, Valanjambalam, Ernakulam 682 016, Kochi, Kerala
  Ph: +91-484-4059061-65,67 Fax: +91-484-4059065 e-mail: kochi@cbspd.com
- **Kolkata:** No. 6/B, Ground Floor, Rameswar Shaw Road, Kolkata-700014 (West Bengal), India
  Ph: +91-33-2289-1126, 2289-1127, 2289-1128 e-mail: kolkata@cbspd.com
- **Mumbai:** 83-C, Dr E Moses Road, Worli, Mumbai-400018, Maharashtra
  Ph: +91-22-24902340/41 Fax: +91-22-24902342 e-mail: mumbai@cbspd.com

Representatives

- **Hyderabad** 0-9885175004
- **Jharkhand** 0-9811541605
- **Nagpur** 0-9021734563
- **Patna** 0-9334159340
- **Pune** 0-9623451994
- **Uttarakhand** 0-9716462459

Printed at Chamc rises, Daryaganj, India

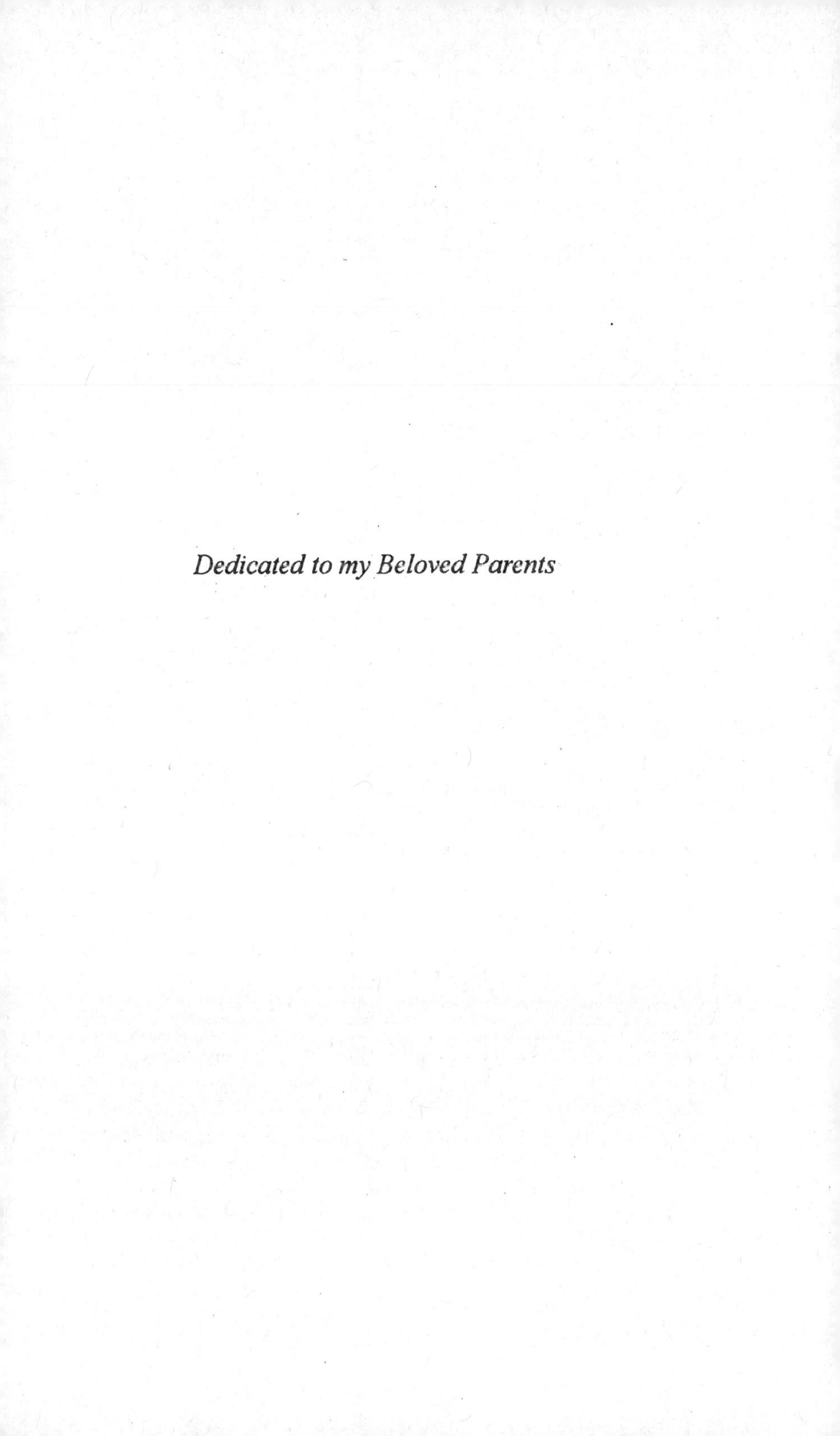

Dedicated to my Beloved Parents

Preface

Now a days AIR POLLUTION is a widely discussed subject, because of the seriousness of the problem. Scientists and engineers need to know about the basic fundamentals of air pollution. Recognising this need, organisations like University Grants Commission and All India Council of Technical Education granted permission to the various universities to start courses on ENVIRONMENTAL SCIENCES AND ENGINEERING at under-graduate and post-graduate levels. To facilitate teaching of these courses it has become necessary to develop text books on environmental sciences including air pollution.

Towards this end an attempt has been made to write a text book on FUNDAMENTALS OF AIR POLLUTION, which is suitable for students. Emphasis has been given to engineering applications.

In this context, I deeply indebted for my friends, colleagues,university authorities and family members for their help, encouragement and co-operation extended in completing this work.

Acknowledgements

The following organisations have kindly premitted to reproduce the material as mentioned in the text.

1) NEERI (National Environmental Engineering Research Institute, Nagpur, India)
2) WHO, NewYork
3) Bureau of Indian Standards, New Delhi
4) McGraw-Hill Kogakusha, New Delhi

Contents

CHAPTER 1

Introduction of Air Pollution

1.1 INTRODUCTION

Air is one of the five essentials (air, water, food, heat, and light) for the human beings. Man breaths nearly 22,000 times in a day and inhales approximately 15kg of air per day. Generally human beings can live for 5 weeks without any food, 5 days without any water but not even 5 minutes without air. Even though the air is abundantly available over the surface of the earth, but it contains lot of impurities. All the impurities in the inhaled air do not cause injury to health and it depends on several factors. The chemical composition of clean atmospheric dry air is given in Table 1.1(a) and comparison of clean air and polluted air in Table 1.1(b). Due to industrialisation in a region, the purity of air has been reducing in that locality to a level which endanger the health of the community.

Table 1.1(a). Chemical composition of clean dry atmospheric air

Substance	Concentration	
	% by volume	by ppm
Nitrogen	78.09	780,900
Oxygen	20:95	209,500
Argon	0.93	9,300
Carbon dioxide	0.032	320
Neon	0.0018	18
Helium	0.00052	5.2
Methane		1.2
Krypton		0.5
Hydrogen		0.5
Xenon		0.08
Nitrogendioxide		0.02
Ozone, etc.		0.01 to 0.04

Table 1.1(b). Comparison of clean air and polluted air

Pollutant	Clean air (ppm)	Polluted air (ppm)
SO_2	0.001–0.01	0.02–2.0
CO_2	310–330	350–700
CO	<1.0	5–200
NO_x	0.001–0.01	0.01–0.5
HC	1.0	1–20
Particulates ($\mu g/m^3$)	10–20	70–700

Various types of contaminants are entering into the atmosphere, by natural and man-made activities which are taking place on the earth. So, in general, air pollution means the presence of a foreign matter in air. Various authors defined 'air pollution' which are as follows.

Dean. E.Painter defined 'air pollution' as the presence in the outdoor atmosphere of one or more contaminants in a sufficient quantity and duration to cause them to be injurious to human health and welfare and animal and plant life and to interfere with the enjoyment of life and property.

The American Medical Association, Council of Industrial Health (WHO) defined 'air pollution' as the excessive concentration of foreign matter in the air which adversely affects the well being of the individual or causes damage to property.

The Bureau of Indian Standards (IS:4167) states that the pollution is the presence in ambient atmosphere of substances generally resulting from the activities of man, in sufficient concentration present for a sufficient time and under circumstances which interfere significantly with the comfort health or welfare of persons or with the full use of enjoyment of property.

A typical legal definition of air pollution is the presence in the outdoor atmosphere of substances or contaminants put there by man, in quantities or concentrations and of a duration as to cause any; discomfort to a substantial number of inhabitants of a district of which are injurious to public health or to human, plant or animal life or property or which interfere with the reasonable comfortable enjoyment of life and property throughout the state or throughout such territories or areas of the state as shall be affected thereby (WHO).

From the above definition, air pollution definition may be simplified as the presence of pollutants in air in sufficient quantity and duration which adversely affect the health and enjoyment of property of human beings, animals and plants.

1.2 EPISODES OF AIR POLLUTION DISASTERS

Episode is an event in the chain of events.

Disaster is a sudden misfortune or a terrible accident.

Air pollution is not a recent phenomenon and the problem of air pollution has existed for centuries. Smoke, ash, sulphurdioxide and other products of combustion have been recognized as nuisance. In 1272, smoke was considered as first air pollutants and King Edward I of England banned the use of sea coal since it released lot of smoke during burning. Henry V (1413–1422) of England regulated the use of coal as fuel. In the year 1800 hydrochloric acid was recognised as atmospheric pollutant (the strong emission of hydrochloric acid was resulted in the production of soda ash from common salt).

In 1961, Royal Command of Charles II published a pamphlet on 'air pollution' and it was recognised that coal was responsible for the unpleasant smell and irritation to the throat and nose.

Air Pollution Disasters

Air pollution disasters occurred in various places in the world. Some of them are severe and a few of them are given below.

1. Meuse Valley (Belgium)

In December, 1930 a heavily industrialised area of Meuse Valley experienced a severe 3-day fog and temperature inversion. In 24 km long Meuse Valley consists of hills on either side with a height of 80 to 120 m, which are occupied by steel and power plants, sulphuric acid plants, and zinc plants. Pollutants got trapped on the valley over a period of three days due to temperature inversion. Due to severe fog 60 people died and several hundred became ill and suffered with eye and nosal irritation. Cattle became sick. .

2. Donora (U.S.A.)

Donora, Pennsylvania is located at 45 km south of Pittsburgh in a horse shoe shaped valley on the Monongahela river. In the last week of October 1948, anticyclone weather condition characterised by little or no air movement occured over a period of 4 days. Temperature inversion and fog resulted the death of 20 people and 6000 out of 14,000 population became ill due to respiratory tract diseases and irritation of eyes.

3. London (England)

From 5th to 9th of December 1952, an anticyclone weather created a subsidence inversion and fog formed over the London area. Due to low temperature inversion, stagnant air, smoke and sulphurdioxide. 4000 people died and several thousands hospitalised for respiratory troubles. Similarly in January, 1956 and December, 1962 air pollution disasters took place in London and hundreds of people died.

4. Los Angeles (U.S.A.)

The city of Los Angeles is located along the narrow pacific coastal plain in the southern portion of State of California. The land rises gradually from the coast line to eastward mountains which are at a height of 600 m over a distance of 50 km. The obnoxious gases released from thousands of automobiles were trapped due to stable atmosphere. The temperature inversion increased the concentration of exhaust gases of automobiles, which resulted the formation of photochemical smog and peroxyl acetyl nitrate (PAN), and experienced a severe smog problem in 1945. It resulted the reduction of visibility, irritation to eyes and damage to vegetation.

5. Tokyo (Japan)

In the early morning of June 18th, 1970, a thick fog was formed over the Tokyo city, due to increased levels of oxidants in the atmosphere. 6000 people suffered with eye irritation, sore throat and difficulty in breathing. Photochemical oxidant reacted with sulphur dioxide resulted acid mist which caused eye irritation.

6. Bhopal (India)

In the early morning hours of 3rd December, 1984, 30 tonnes of deadly methyl iso cynate (MIC) gas was released from storage tank due to alleged failure of vent scrubber system. More than 2500 deaths occured and one lakh people severely affected with coughing, conjunctivities, suffocation and cardiac failure.

It is observed the following points from the above air pollution disasters.

(i) Majority of air pollution disasters were occured during late night or early hours of winter months, because the dispersion of pollutants is low.

(ii) The situations were triggered due to heavy accumulation of air pollutants, which were released from huge processed industries, where they were located in a centralised area.

(iii) The worst conditions occured in a U-shaped vallies or hilly terrains.

(iv) In some occasion even the industries were located in the plain areas, the disasters took place due to failure of necessary checks for leakages and safety measures.

Hence, to avoid the disasters or atleast to minimise them, proper attention is necessary by the authorities to consider topographical, meteorological, man and environment, and safety maintenance aspects while locating the industries. In this regard, it is always desirable to remember and remind the slogan of "PREVENTION IS ALWAYS BETTER THAN CURE".

CHAPTER 2

Sources and Classification of Air Pollutants

2.1 SOURCES OF AIR POLLUTANTS

Pollutants present in air may be in the form of solids, liquids and gases which are produced by natural and man-made activities. Naturally occurring processes like dust storms, volcanic eruptions etc. create pollution. Man-made activities like industries and civil construction operations also generate pollution. For the convenience of study, various sources of air pollution are classified which are as follows

Type-I Classification

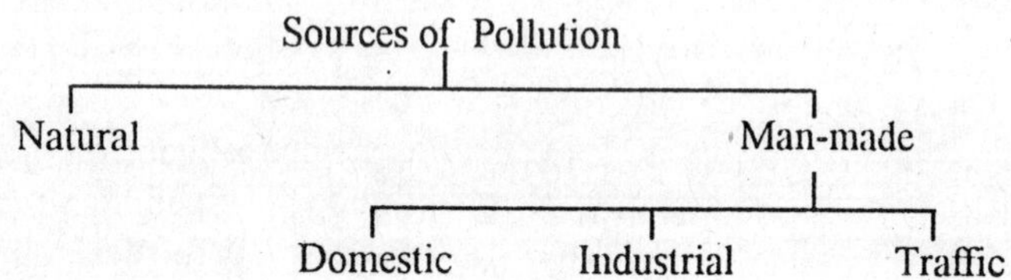

Natural Sources

Dust Storms: Dust storms are produced due to wind circulation around the planet Earth. Global meteorological processes makes the environment with dust pollution, in some areas and in some occasions.

Forest Fires: Huge quantities of smoke (carbon particles) are liberated during forest fires.

Volcanoes: Volcanoes (eruption of lava from earth's core) release lot of solid particles, gases like sulphur dioxide and radiation. Heat waves may be spread up to several kilometers. The surrounding areas are greatly affected with heavy dust and heat pollution.

Sea Spray: Sea spray is a continuous phenomena, which is a major source of particulate (liquid droplets) pollution in the atmosphere.

Plant Pollen: During spring season, lot of plant pollen is produced and due to wind motion, it is spread very fastly, which makes the atmosphere with dust pollution.

Many gaseous carbon compounds such as methane, carbondioxide, carbonmonoxide, etc are emitted into atmosphere through biological processes, volcanic eruptions, forest fires, natural gas seepage.

The pollution due to natural sources is a continuous phenomenon and more or less it is constant in the planet Earth, because of its cyclic natural processes. This pollution is very significant comparing with man-made pollution. But in the nature, there are several self-purification mechanisms which makes the planet Earth sustainable for the living world. Man's role is very less to control the natural sources of pollution. But he can aggrevate the pollution by disturbing natural and ecological balances due to man-made polhution.

Man-made Sources

Domestic Pollution: It is generated by the domestic or household activities or infections or using insecticides for cleaning and maintenance of houses. Even though it is not significant comparing with other sources, but it contributes to affect the quality of municipal sewage. Good house keeping methods may help to reduce the pollution.

Industrial Pollution: It is a major pollution generated by the man-made activities. Among the industries, thermal power plants, chemical plants, cement plants, paper mills, textile mills and tanneries etc. are the major sources of pollution. Adopting proper pollution control methods will help to reduce the pollution at sources.

Traffic Pollution: It is considered as serious as industrial pollution because of rapid and unplanned urbanisation. The pollution produced by the traffic may be in the form of exhaust gases, particulates and noise etc. This pollution may be minimised by adopting city, regional and country planning methods, using good fuels and automobiles with pollution control technology.

However, EPA (Environmental Protection Agency) has classified the principal sources of air pollution, which are as follows.

(a) Transportation, e.g.: ships, aeroplanes, trains and automobiles.

(b) Fuel combustion from stationery sources, e.g: power plants etc.

(c) Industrial process, e.g.: steel mills, textile mills, and paper mills

(d) Solid waste disposal, e.g.: open burning, incineration and sanitary land fills, and

(e) Miscellaneous processes, e.g.: domestic activities like insecticide cleaning.

Type-II Classification

Based on the shape of entry of pollutants into the atmosphere, the source of pollutants may be classified into three types, which are as follows:

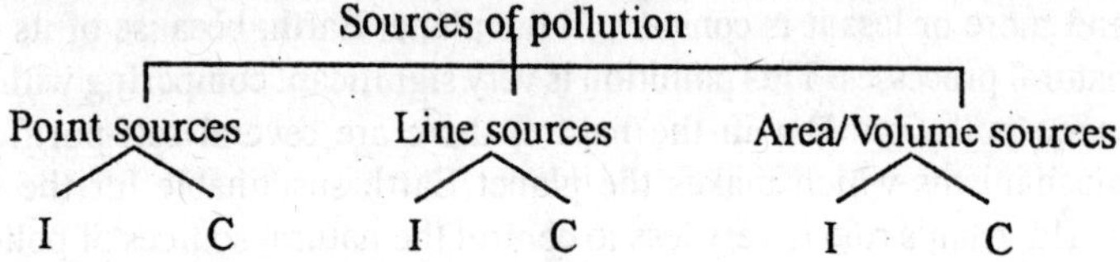

where

I = Instantaneous sources and C = Continuous sources

Instantaneous point source means 'puff' (small volume) of material is released into the atmosphere in a relatively short time. e.g.: nuclear explosion, volcanic eruption.Continuous point source means the polluted gas coming out continuously from a point (relatively small diameter) e.g. : release of smoke from a stack of power plant, etc.

Instantaneous line source means the pollutants dispersion into the atmosphere from a source which has a 'line' shape at a time, e.g. : pesticides spray path while emitted by aeroplanes. Continuous line source means the pollutants dispersion into the atmosphere from a line source continuously, e.g.: urban heavy traffic road.

Instantaneous area/volume source means the entry of pollutants into the atmosphere from an area/volume (relatively large comparing with a point source) at a time instant, e.g.: blasting of poisonous gas tank. Continuous area/volume source means the entry of pollutants into the atmosphere form an area/volume continuously, e.g.: heart of urban city complex, or area/volume of an industrial park.

This type of classification of sources of pollution will be useful in air pollution modelling studies of dispersion of pollutants.

2.2 FACTOR AFFECTING AIR POLLUTION

The factor which affect air pollution are as follows.

(i) Meteorological characteristics

Meteorological parameters like wind direction and magnitude, atmospheric lapse rates and relative humidity, etc. of a locality will influence the air pollution. Wind velocity and direction will carry the pollutant by advection (pollution carried by downwind velocity). The ground level concentrations are mostly depended on wind direction and magnitude and lapse rates. The mixing depth for the dispersion of pollutants is depended on lapse rates. The temperature variation with height will make the pollutants to move less or more speed.

Relative humidity is another important parameter which will influence temperture variations in a region. If temperature is more near the earth's surface, water vapour will be more in the atmosphere (particularly in troposphere). Hence, relative humidity is more. It absorbs earth's re-radiation and hold it in the troposphere (upto 2 km above the earth's surface). These changes will influence the dispersion of pollutants in the atmosphere.

(ii) Topographical features

The dispersion of pollutants are affected by the unevenness of the land forms and barriers (obstacles) like mountains, etc. Topographical features will be advantageous and disadvantageous depending on the occasion and local conditions. These affects have been discussed in detail in Chapter 5 (Meteorology and Air Pollution).

(iii) Characteristics of pollutants

The seriousness of air pollution problems are depended on the type and size of pollutants, either solid, liquid or gas. It may be also due to energy, either noise, or heat or radioactive, or combination of above. The interaction of pollutants in the atmosphere may reduce or increase the level of pollution, which is depended upon the characteristics of the pollutants.

(iv) Mode of release of pollutants

The affect of air pollution is depended upon the way of entry of pollutants and also rate of release of pollutants. They may be released intermittently or continuous or cyclic or from a single source or from multiple sources or point and non-point sources. The dispersion of pollutants is also depended upon the mode of release of pollutants into the atmosphere.

The detailed discussion about the factors which will influence the air pollution has been covered in Chapter 5.

2.3 CLASSIFICATION OF AIR POLLUTANTS

Air pollutants may be broadly classified which are as follows:

A. Based on the Origin of Pollutants

(i) Primary pollutants: Primary pollutants are the pollutants which are emitted directly into the atmosphere from the sources, e.g. release of sulphur dioxide by burning of coal.

(ii) Secondary pollutants: Secondary pollutants are the pollutants which are formed due to the interaction of two or more primary pollutants or a result of some reaction with normal atmospheric constituents with or with out photoactivation, e.g. ozone (nitrogenoxide + $O_2 \longrightarrow O_3$).

B. Based on the Chemical Composition

(i) Organic pollutants, e.g.: Hydrocarbons
(ii) Inorganic pollutants, e.g.: CO, SO_2, SO_3, H_2S

C. Based on the State of Matter

(i) Particulate pollutants: Particulate pollutants are finely divided solid or liquid particles. Particulates can be composed of inert or extremely reactive materials of size from 0.0002 (small molecule) to 500 microns. (1micron = 10^{-6} m, e.g.: dust, smoke, fumes etc).

(ii) Gaseous pollutants: Gaseous pollutants are the pollutants which are present in the form of gas e.g.: SO_2, H_2S

Based on the size, the particulate matter may be classified which are as follows:

Aerosols: Aerosols are nothing but air suspensions. The particles suspended may be dust, smoke, mist, and fumes. This is a most general term applied to any tiny particles, either liquid or solids, dispersed in the atmosphere.

Dust: It is a air suspension of irregular shaped mineral or other particles of size 1 to 200 microns. They settle under the influence of gravity. It is generated by crushing, chipping, grinding and by natural disintegration of rock and soil. Particles of this size range will be in the suspended state from, a few seconds to several months. If the size is less than 100 microns, it is called as fine dust and greater than 100 microns called as coarse dust. Particles of size greater than 50 microns can be seen with unaided eye. The typical sizes of dusts are given below.

Dust particles of crushing and grinding	>20	microns
Fly ash from chimney	3 – 80	"
Cement dust	10 – 150	"
Foundry dust	1 – 200	"

Smoke: It is an aerosol of very fine carbon particles of size range from 0.5 to 1.0 micron which are produced by incomplete combustion of organic particles such as coal, wood etc.

Soot: Soot is agglomeration of carbon particles of size 1 to 10 microns impregnated with tar, formed due to incomplete combustion of carbonaceous materials.

Fumes: Fumes are the fine solid particles formed by condensation of gaseous state after volatisation. The size range of particles is 0.03 to 1 micron.

Mist: Mist is an aerosol of liquid droplets formed by the condensation of vapour. The size range of natural water vapour mists are from 40 to 500 microns. Usually the size is less than 10 μ.

Fog: Water mist is called fog. It is the mist in which the liquid is water (sufficiently dense to obscure visibility). It is a visible aerosol.

Smog: Smoke plus fog is expressed as smog.

Spray: It consists of liquid droplets formed by the atomization of parent liquids (pesticides). The size of particles range from 10 to 1000 microns.

Haze: Haze is an air pollution condition (decrease in the visibility in atmosphere) formed due to presence of very fine dust, mist etc. in the atmosphere. Haze is expressed as Coefficient of Haze (COH) which is defined as follows.

$$\text{COH} = 100 \log_{10} \left(\frac{100}{\%\ \text{Transmittance}} \right)$$

Gas: Gas is a matter which is having neither independent shape or volume and tending to expand indefinitely.

Vapour: Gaseous phase of matter which normally exist in a liquid or solid state.

Based on the chemical composition inorganic gaseous pollutants are classified as follows.

Type	Primary	Secondary
(i) Sulphur compouds	SO_2, H_2S	SO_3, H_2SO_4
(ii) Nitrogen compounds	NO, NH_3	NO_2, HNO_3
(iii) (a) Carbon oxides	CO, CO_2	None
(b) Carbon containing compounds	C_1–C_5	aldehydes, ketones
(iv) Fluoride compounds	HF	None
(v) Oxidants	None	O_3

Sulphur Compounds: Coal, oil contains sulphur as impurity. Sulphur content of coal varies 1 to 5% . When fuel is burned, the sulphur also burns producing sulphur dioxide gas and also sulphur trioxide gas. They are the dominant oxides of sulphur present in the atmosphere.

SO_2: The most important oxide emitted by pollution sources is sulphur dioxide. It is a coulourless, nonflammable, nonexplosive gas. It cause a taste sensation at concentrations from 0.3 to 1.0 ppm in air . At concentrations greater than 3 ppm, the SO_2 gas has a pungent irritating odour. It is partly converted to sulphur trioxide or sulphuric acid and its salts by photochemical or catalytic processes in the atmosphere. In a polluted atmosphere SO_2 reacts photo-chemically or catalytically with other pollutants. Sulphurdioxide gas alone can irritate the upper respiratory tract and it can be carried deep into lungs.

Sulphur trioxide: It is generally emitted along with sulphur dioxide (1 to 5 % concentration). SO_3 rapidly combines with moisture in the atmosphere and form sulphuric acid. Both SO_2 and SO_3 are washed from the atmosphere during raining.

H_2S. Hydrogen sulphide is a foul smelling gas produced during anaerobic biological decomposition and also from kraft pulp plants, etc.

Nitrogen Compounds: The oxides of nitrogen (NO, NO_2) are the primary pollutants released by petroleum operations industrial and automobile combustion. There are seven oxides of nitrogen (N_2O, NO, NO_2, NO_3, N_2O_3, N_2O_4, and N_2O_5) in which three oxides namely nitrous oxide (N_2O) nitric oxide (NO) and nitorgen dioxide (NO_2) are formed in the atmosphere. Generally NO and NO_2 are analysed together and referred as NO_x.

Nitrous Oxide(N_2O): Nitrous oxide is a colourless, odourless gas commonly present in the atmosphere (0.25 ppm in concentration), which is released due to biological activity of the soil. It is also called as laughing gas and anesthetic.

Nitric oxide (NO): It is also a colourless, odourless gas which forms under high temperature combustion processess. It is not a pollutant and inert at normal atmospheric condition. It is oxidised to nitrogendioxide (NO_2) in a polluted atmosphere through photochemical reaction. NO is emitted into the large quantities by automobiles than NO_2. It is formed in combustion process with high temperature.

$$N_2 + O_2 \longrightarrow NO$$

NO in atmosphere readily oxidised to NO_2

Nitrogen Dioxide(NO_2): It is a brown pungent gas with a irritating odour. It is corrosive to materials and toxic to man. It absorbs sunlight energy (ultra violet range) and initiates photochemical reactions that produce smog. It is emitted by fuel combustion and nitric acid plants. It is heavier than air and it is readily soluble in water which forms nitrous acid and nitricoxide.

$$2NO_2 + H_2O \longrightarrow HNO_3 + HNO_2$$

$$3NO_2 \quad \text{ч}_2 \longrightarrow 2HNO_3 + NO$$

Both combine with ammonia in the atmosphere and form ammonium nitrate and fall with rain.

Carbon Compounds: Carbonmonoxide is a primary pollutant which is colourless, odourless and tasteless gas. It is mainly originated from incomplete combustion of fuels (carbonaceous materials), especially due to automobile exhausts. It is highly poisonous gas and is generally considered as an asphyxiant. Carbonmonoxide is present in small concentration in the atmosphere with a life time of 2 to 4 months, The toxicity of carbonmonoxide is due to its affinity for haemoglobin which is the oxygen carrier of the blood. It is non-toxic to insects and other forms of life which have no red blood cells. CO has no detrimental effects on material surfaces and vegetation.

CO_2: Carbondioxide is also produced along with carbonmonoxide, but it is not considered as pollutant. Burning of fossil fuels such as coal, oil, and natural gas releases carbondioxide, which is accumulating over the earth from the past 500 million years. These huge man-made emissions have been entering the atmosphere faster than the natural cycle (carbondioxide → air and dissolved water → plants → animals → carbondioxide). The temperature of the earth's surface increases when the carbondioxide in the atmosphere increases, because CO_2 strongly absorbs long wave (Infrared) terrestrial radiation and continued CO_2 build up, traps heat and prevents some of it to re-radiate back in to space.

In the natural cycle, carbondioxide is uniformly distributed upto 75 km over the earth surface. About half of the extra carbondioxide produced by combustion of hydrocarbons is retained in the atmosphere. As per the projections of the some investigators, by 2000 A.D. carbondioxide increases 125 % of 1850 level, which is sufficient to produce significant changes in climate.

Hydrocarbons: These are the primary pollutants released into the atmosphere in petroleum production and incomplete combustion of fuels like gasoline, diesel etc. The gaseous and volatile liquid hydrocarbons are the major air pollutants in the atmosphere. Their presence in air alone are not harmful. They undergo chemical reactions in the presence of sunlight and nitrogen oxides forming photochemical oxidants.

Derived hydrocarbons such as aldehydes, carbon tetrachloride etc. may be released as primary pollutants and also secondary pollutants in the certain conditions .

Fluoride Compounds: Fluorine is very toxic and corrosive substance when it is present in elemental state. Generally it is not present in atmosphere as air pollutant . But fluorides may be found in the atmosphere as gaseous or as a particulate matter. The typical fluoride compounds are given below.

Compound	As pollutant	Formula	Solubility
Hydrogen fluoride	gas – liquid	HF	water soluble
Silicon tetrafluoride	gas – liquid	SiF_4	water soluble
Hydrofluosilicic Acid	gas – liquid	H_2SiF_6	water soluble
Sodium fluoride	solid	NaF	water soluble
Sodium aluminum silicofluoride	solid	$Na_3Al(SiF_6)_4$	water soluble
Sodium silicofluoride	solid	Na_2SiF_6	Slightly soluble
Aluminum fluoride	solid	AlF_3	slightly soluble
Fluorapatite	solid	$CaFCa_4(PO_4)_2$	slightly soluble
Cryolite	solid	Na_3AlF_6	water insoluble
Fluorspar, fluoride	solid	CaF_2	water insoluble

All fluoride containing compounds are likely to be chemically reactive and in unpolluted atmosphere, the concentration of fluorides is very low. But, fluoride-emitting industries substantially contribute fluorides to the surrounding area. Industries such as fertilizer, aluminium, steel,etc.utilise fluoride-containing compounds and release as fluorides along with other waste gases in to the atmosphere. Silicon tetrafluoride (SiF_4) and gaeous hydrogen fluoride are the primary pollutants which are emitted mainly from fertilizer industry. Phosphate rocks which may contain 2–4% fluorides while processing with strong sulphuric acid, volatile hydrogen fluoride and silicon tetra fluoride gases are significantly emitted into the atmosphere. Calcium or sodium fluorides are used in steel industry, which are added to molten steel to release gaseous products. Fluorides will come out as gaseous effluents along with other exhausts.

Other Pollutants: As per the Environmental protection Agency (EPA),USA the following elements and radicals etc. is being considered as air pollutants and measuring as a part of air quality surveillance programme.

Elements	Radicals	Gases	Others
Antimony	Ammonium	Carbon monoxide	Aero allergens
Arsenic	Fluoride	Methane	Asbestoes
Barium	Nitrate	Nitric oxide	β-radioactivity
Beryllium	Sulphate	Nitrogen dioxide	Benzene soluble organic compounds
Bismuth		Pesticide	Benzo pyrene
Boron		Sulphur dioxide	Pesticides
Cadmium		Reactive hydrocarbons	Suspended particulate matter
Chromium		Total hydrocarbons	
Cobalt		Total oxidants	
Copper			
Iron			
Lead			
Manganese			
Mercury			
Molybdenum			
Nickel			
Selenium			
Tin			
Titanium			
Vanadium			
Zinc			

SHORT/FILL UP THE BLANK TYPE QUESTIONS

1. Sulphur forms a number of oxides (SO, SO_2, S_2O_3, SO_3, S_2O_7) but only SO_2 and SO_3 are very important as gaseous air pollutants.
2. SO_2 rapidly combines with water in air to form H_2SO_4 which has a low dew point.
3. What are the sulphur compounds other than SO_2 which are interested to air pollution because of their strong odours?
   Methyl mercaptan and dimethyl sulphide
4. *Ozone* is a bluish gas secondary air pollutant which is 1.6 times as heavy as air and forms at high altitudes by photochemical reactions.

5. Man consumes 1.5 kg of food, 2.5 kg of water and 15 kg of air per day.
6. Approximately one tone of coal needs 12 tons of air for combustion.
7. Earth's temperature is increasing approximately 0.5 °C decade due to natural and man made activities.
8. *CO* is produced as a product of incomplete combustion of carbon and its compounds.
9. Oxides of sulphur *(SO_2, SO_3, and H_2S)* result from the combustion of coal and oil for domestic, industrial and transportation.
10. Oxides of sulphur combines with moisture in the air and produce sulphuric acid as *secondary* pollutant.
11. Oxides of *nitrogen* result from automobile, industrial combustion and petroleum refineries.
12. Incomplete combustion of fuels and fuming of metals oxides produce *CO* and CO_2
13. CO is a crucial pollutant, and CO_2 is not a pollutant in general.
14. *Chlorine* is a heavy yellowish coloured gas which is having a strong pungent odour.
15. *Ammonia* is a considered to be a relatively unimportant pollutant gas which has a sharp odour and it can be detected by taste at 20 ppm.
16. CO_2, water vapour and ozone concentration increase will change the *absorption* and *transmission* characteristics of the atmosphere.
17. In the presence of sunlight, hydrocarbons react with oxides of nitrogen and form *photochemical smog.*
18. $CO + Cl_2 \longrightarrow$ *Phosgene* (poisonous gas)
19. Phosgene + methyl amine $\longrightarrow$ Methyl Iso-cyanate (MIC).
20. Power plants are the major source of SO_2 gaseous pollutant.
21. Typical coal contained 1 to 3% of sulphur.
22. 2% of sulphur coal will produce 40 kg of SO_2 per ton of coal burned.
23. Burning of natural gas produces negligible SO_x, CO and HC, and produce a very significant quantity of the *oxides of nitrogen.*
24. Bhopal gas tragedy took place on early *morning of 3rd December (second night) 1984.*
25. CO_2 is less soluble at higher *temperature.*
26. Aerosols are finely divided *liquid* droplets or *solid* particles.
27. Acid mist reduces *visibility.*
28. Every Kg of copper produced in copper smelters *2 Kg* SO_2 is produced.
29. The sources that contribute to the creation of air pollution are both *natural* and *man-made.*
30. Oxygen atoms may be split from nitrogen oxides to combine with oxygen in the atmosphere to form *ozone*, a *secondary pollutant.*
31. Particulate air pollutants size range from *0.0002* to *500* microns.
32. One micron is *1/1000* mm.
33. Fumes and smoke are particulates in the size range from *0.1 to 1.0 microns.*
34. Soot is the particulate pollutant in the range of *1 to 10* microns.
35. Particles larger than *one micron* tend to settle out of the atmosphere.
36. Hydrochloric acid is a secondary *pollutant* which may be produced by hydrolysis of *hydrogen chloride gas.*
37. According to EPA (Environmental Protection Agency), the principal sources of air pollution are *transportation, fuel combustion from stationary sources, industrial processes and solid waste disposal.*
38. The aerosols formed during the chemical reactions that create smog cause a marked reduction in visibility and give atmosphere a *brownish cast.*

39. Continued discharge of *particulate matter* into atmosphere will decrease in temperature and lead to another ice age.
40. List of three domestic sources of air pollution: 1. *Fuel burning like cooking gas,* 2. *Fire wood,* 3. *Waste paper burning (incineration).*
41. Bhopal gas tragedy is because of *Methyl Iso-Cyanate (MIC)* pollutant.
42. Define air pollution: Presence of pollutants in air in sufficient quantity and duration, which adversely effect the health and enjoyment of property of human beings, animals and plants.
43. What is CFC ? Why it is an air pollutant ?
    CFC means chloro fluorocarbons. From the industries, and as refrigerant, it enters into the atmosphere and reaches into the top of the atmosphere and ozone layer. It creates holes in the ozone layer.
44. Expand MIC-*Methyl Iso-Cyanate.*
45. "Approximately One ton of coal needs 12 tons air for combustion" substantiate?
    $C + O_2 \longrightarrow CO_2$
    (12 32 44), so one part of carbon requires 32/12 = 2.66 parts of oxygen, and 2.66/0.21 = 12.38 parts of air, since the oxygen in air is 21%.
46. SO_3 can react with moisture in the air to produce H_2SO_4.
47. Expand PAN-Peroxy Acetyl Nitrate.
48. SO_2 pollutant, is damaging the beauty of Taj Mahal.
49. Major air pollutants from a thermal power station are *fly ash and* SO_2.
50. Smoke is given out of wood, coal, tobacco because of *incomplete combustion.*
51. The colourless, odourless, tasteless gas that effects warm blooded animals and no impact on the insects, vegetation and metallic surfaces is *carbonmonoxide.*
52. Atmospheric temperature rises because of the release of *carbondioxide.*
53. SO_2 gas in the atmosphere results acid rain.
54. *Ozone or PAN* is a secondary air pollutant.
55. N_2O *(Nitrous oxide)* gas has anaesthetic property, and used in minor surgery and dentistry.
56. Brown discolouration of the sky occurs becaue of excess concentration of NO_2 in the atmosphere.
57. As per the EPA, out of the major sources of air pollution a proportion (ratio) of about *15:100* can be attributed to industrial processes.
58. Smoke and fog together make up *smog.*
59. Thunder storms are found *more* or less frequently in the heavily polluted areas than in non polluted areas.
60. Rise in rainfall levels can be correlated with *particulates (SPM)* pollution levels.
61. NO of NO_x are formed when combustion take place at high *temperature* and also by fixation of nitrogen and oxygen.
62. *NO* of NO_x is not an irritant and also not considered to have adverse health effects at normal atmospheric concentrations.
63. The danger of NO is related to its formation as NO_2 which is an air pollutant.
64. *Sulphur* oxides are produced mainly by burning of coal and fuel oil.
65. Inorganic photochemical oxidants *ozone and* NO_2 are produced by the radiant energy of the sun, changing primary pollutants into secondary pollutants by various reactions.
66. *Soot* is the carbonaceous particles and minute tar droplets which are discharged as a result of incomplete combustion of fuels and other compounds containing carbons.
67. Dispersed liquid droplets or solid particles suspended in the air are called *aerosol.*

68. *CO* is an odourless, tasteless and colourless gas, which is slightly lighter than air.
69. NO_2 is brownish red colour pungent irritating, odourous gas, in oxides of nitrogen.
70. Every year the concentration of carbon dioxide is increasing in the troposphere at the rate of *0.3 to 0.5* ppm.
71. Peroxy benzyl nitrate (PBN) is a *secondary* pollutant.
72. A part of the solar rays is highly reflected back by desert sands, snow and ice where as *forests and cultivated fields* have a low rate of reflection.
73. *Nitrous oxide* (N_2O) is a colourless, slightly sweet, non–toxic gas present in the natural environment in relatively large amounts.
74. *Nitric oxide (NO)* is a colourless, odourless and tasteless gas, which associate to form secondary pollutant in atmosphere.
75. *Nitric oxide* gas in air is oxidized rapidly by atmospheric ozone and photochemical process and, more slowly by oxygen to form nitrogen dioxide.
76. *Carbon dioxide* gas contributes "green-house" effect in the atmosphere.
77. 0.0002 μm < fume < 1 μm < dust < 76 μm < mist < 500 μm.
78. NO_2 *(an oxide of nitrogen)* is a strong absorbent of ultra violet light from the sun and forms smog with smoke.
79. Rise in CO_2 concentration increases earth's surface temperature and Arctic ice caps may get melted.
80. *Fumes* are fine solid particles formed by the condensation of vapours of solid material.
81. *Argon* occupies the next place after Nitrogen and oxygen in the free unpolluted atmosphere.
82. While the sulphuric acid is the secondary pollutant, its primary pollutant is *sulphur dioxide.*
83. The chemical that killed more than 3,000 people of Bhopal is *MIC.*
84. Because of excess smoke Sun's rays are prevented from reaching the earth depriving children of vitamin D which leads to a disease called *emotional health in the darkened environments.*
85. Smoke is the product of the incomplete *combustion.*
86. pH of natural lakes is reduced to as low a value as 4 because of *carbondioxide* gas.
87. *Nitrous oxide* (N_2O) is called laughing gas.
88. *Hydrocarbons* + O_2 + NO_2 sunlight ⟶ PAN + O_3.
89. The most common air pollutant formed at the time of bursting of volcanoes as well as during burning of coal is *smoke.*
90. *Fluorine* gas is emitted out of the stacks of aluminium smelters.
91. *Oxidants* are any oxygen containing substance that react chemically in the air to produce new substances.
92. Ozone layer depletion takes place due to the presence of *chloro fluoro carbon (CFC* compounds in the atmosphere.
93. *Ozone, PAN* are secondary pollutants and are formed by photochemical reactions involving the primary pollutants emitted into auto mobile exhaust.
94. World's tallest chimney was built in Ontario, Canada of height of *380 m.*
95. *Sulphurdioxide* is a colourless, non-flammable, non-explosive gas with pungent irritating and suffocating odour which acts either as a reducing or an oxidising agent.
96. *Oxidants like ozone* causes premature aging, reduction in body fat content and affects vision.
97. "2% of sulphur coal will produce 40 kg of sulphurdioxide per ton of coal burning" how?

$S + O_2 \longrightarrow SO_2$

32 32 64 which means 1 part of sulphur gives two parts of sulphurdioxide, 2% of sulphur coal of one ton contain 20 kg. of sulphur, so one ton of 2% sulphur coal while burning gives 2 x 20 = *40 Kg* of SO_2.

98. Incomplete combustion of fuels produces *CO*, a crucial pollutant.
99. *CO* is a chemical asphyxiant.
100. Define fog? Fog combines with the smoke containing air pollutants is referred as smog.
101. Define primary and secondary pollutants? Pollutants which are emitted directly into the atmosphere from the source. Pollutants which are formed due to interaction of two or more pollutants present in the atmosphere.
102. Photochemical smog means smog formed by photochemical reaction which is caused sby the interaction of some hydrocarbons and oxidants under the influence of sunlight.
103. Which gas which is not an air pollutant causing increase in earth's temperature: *Carbon dioxide.*
104. Expand GEMS: Global Environmental Monitoring Systems
105. Expand UNEP: United Nations Environmental Programme.

CHAPTER 3

Effects of Air Pollution on Human Health, Animals, Plants and Properties

3.1 EFFECTS OF AIR POLLUTION ON HUMAN HEALTH

The effects of air pollution on human beings is mainly on eyes and respiratory system. Air-borne gases, vapours, fumes and dust etc., when they come and contact the organs of the body it causes irritation of eyes, nose, throat, and lungs.

(a) Respiratory System

The respiratory system of human beings is shown in Fig. 3.1.

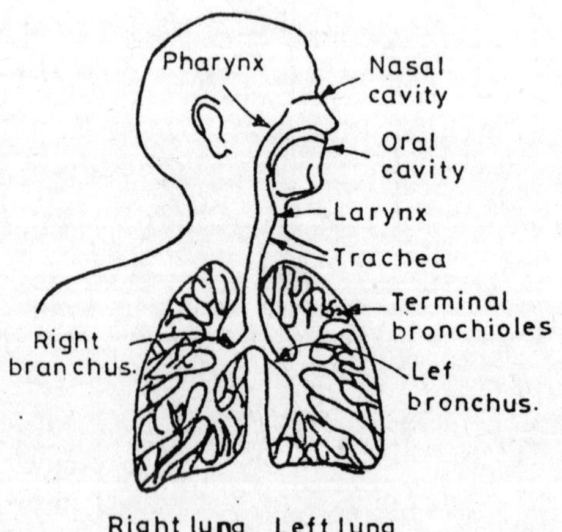

Fig. 3.1.

It consists of lungs and respiratory tract (e.g. tract of air passage from nasal cavity to the lungs). The function of this system is to inhale air into the lungs, filter the impurities from the inhaled air, supply oxygen from the inhaled air to the blood circulatory system and exhale carbon dioxide from the blood through nasal cavity. If the particulate matter inhaled by the human beings, it will be deposited in various regions of the respiratory system depending on the size of particles. If the size is greater than 10 microns, they are retained by the cilia of the nose. If the size is less than 10 microns, they may enter the upper respiratory tract. The upper respiratory tract consists of nasal cavity, nasal pharynx, larynx and trachea. The particles of size 2 to 10 microns may enter upto trachea but the movement of cilia sweeps mucus upward, carrying particles from windpipe to mouth, where they can be swallowed. The lower respiratory tract consists of bronchi, bronchioles, alveolar ducts, alveolar sacs and alveoli of the lungs. Particles of size less than 2 microns are deposited in branchioles but few of them may reach the alveolar ducts. Particles of size less range from 0.25 to 1 microns enter alveoli of lungs and deposit which reduces the volume of the alveoli thereby causing damage to the lungs by minimising the oxygen exchange from air to blood.

(b) The Eye

Eye irritation may result when gaseous or particulate material come and contact the external coat of the eye and the internal mucous line of the eye lid. Irritation of eye leads to rubbing which may cause physical damage. The effect of specific air pollutants on human health are given in Table 3.1.

Inorganic Gases

Carbon Monoxide: Carbon monoxide is a poisonous inhalent. When it is inhaled, it passes through lungs and diffuses into the blood. Carbonmonoxide has a strong affinity for combining with the haemoglobin which is present in the blood. The combination of carbonmonoxide with haemoglobin leads to formation of carboxyhaemoglobin (CoHb). The affinity of haemoglobin to absorb carbonmonoxide is 200 times more than that of oxygen. Therefore, carbonmonoxide will be absorbed into the blood instead of oxygen, which reduces the ability of haemoglobin to carry oxygen to the tissues. Due to lack of oxygen (asphyxiation) death can occur. The ambient air quality standard is 10 ppm. for 8-h exposure. At 100 ppm.

Table 3.1. Effects of specific air pollurtants on human health

Pollutants	Source	Effects
Aldehyde	Auto exhausts	Irritation to eyes, skin
Ammonia	Chemical industries	Corrosive to mucous membrane, damage to eyes
Arsenic	Metal smelters	Damage to skin
Cadmium	Metal industry	Chronic and acute poisoning, kidney, liver damage.
Chlorine	Chemical industry	Irritation to eye and throat
Chromium	Metallurgical and tannery industries	Toxicity to body tissues
Lead	Lead smelters and pesticides, autos	Deposition in lungs, nervous disorders
Mercury	Smlters, paints	Brain and kidney
Nickel	Diesel combustion Tobacco smoke	Lung cancer and respiratory systerr

most people experience dizziness, headache. Cigarette smoke contains 400 to 450 ppm of CO. When the CO concentration is greater than 750 ppm, death can occur for a short period (few minutes) of exposure. At 250 to 500 ppm, people will experience the less of consciousness. Generally in urban busy traffic streets contain CO of concentration of 5 to 20 ppm.

SO_2: Sulphurdioxide can cause irritation, reduction of visibility, respiratory diseases. Healthy persons experience broncho-construction at 1.6 ppm of SO_2 for a few minutes exposure. Throat irritation occurs at 8–12 ppm level. 10 ppm can cause eye irritation. At 20 ppm, immediate cough and eye irritation results. Exposure of 400 to 500 ppm of sulphur dioxide even for a few minutes is dangerous to life. Normally urban air contains 0.001 to 0.2 ppm.

NO_x: Nitricoxide (NO) and Nitrogendioxide (NO_2) are of interest to the concern of human health. NO is not irritant and it will not cause any adverse health effects at atmospheric concentrations. But when NO undergoes oxidation to NO_2, it poses health hazards as oxidant. Haemoglobin has 300,000 times affinity for absorbing NO_2 than O_2, which reduces oxygen carrying capacity of the blood. Nitrogenoxides cause lung tissues to become leathery and brittle and may cause lung cancer and emphysema. Threshold value is 0.12 ppm. of NO_2. Increased air way resistance occurs at 2 to 5 ppm for 1-h exposure. Nitrogen dioxide at high-level exposures of 150 ppm (285 mg/m^3) and above are fatal to humans.

Oxidants: Ozone causes eye irritation when the concentration exceeds 0.1 ppm. Nasal and throat irritation occurs at 0.3 ppm over a period of 8-h exposure. At 1.5 to 2.0 ppm concentrations of 2-h exposure will cause heat pain, coughing and headache. Severe illness will occur at 10 ppm. Photochemical smog consists of air contaminants such as O_3, PAN, PBN (peroxy-benzyl nitrate), aldehydes, ketones etc.

Organic Gases: Gaseous hydrocarbons play a vital role in the formation of photochemical oxidants.

Generally the following diseases may occur due to air pollution:

Lung Cancer: It is nothing but destruction of lung tissue. Organic carcinogens, specific inorganics like arsenic, asbestos, cadmium, chromium, nickel, radioactive materials may cause lung cancer.

Chronic Bronchitis: It is the reduction of efficiency of air delivery by reducing the diameter of the bronchioles.

Bronchial Asthma: More responsiveness of the trachea and the bronchi to various stimuli which will occur by narrowing of the airways.

Emphysema: It is due to progressive breakdown of alveolar air sacs in the lungs by chronic infection or irritation of the bronchial tubes, paralysis of the cilia, injury from violet coughing. Emphysema progressively diminishes the ability of lungs to exchange oxygen and carbon dioxide to blood stream.

3.2. EFFECTS ON ANIMALS

Air pollutants like arsenic, fluorine, lead, molybdenum and selenium will cause acute injury and death.

(i) Arsenic: Arsenic poisoning causes sick in the animals due to the eating of grass with arsenic fall-out. Inflammation of the respiratory, gastro intestinal tract, destruction of red blood cells and kidney damage in cattle, horses and sheeps can occur. Acute poisoning symptoms are salivation, thirst, odour of garlic on the animal's breath. Horses may have ulcers of the nose, difficult breathing.

(ii) Fluorine: Cattle and sheep will be affected to fluorine poisoning (fluorosis). It occurs by ingestion of vegetation with fluoride containing matter.

(iii) Lead: Acute lead poisoned animals give symptoms like foaming at the mouth and damage in the nervous system, etc.

3.3. EFFECTS ON AIR POLLUTION ON VEGETATION

The most frequently affecting air pollutants to vegetation are sulphur dioxide, hydrogen fluoride, ozone, chlorine, PAN, oxides of nitrogen, hydrogen sulphide, ammonia, mercury vapours etc. They mainly attack on stomata and palisade and spongy mesophyll regions of the leaf. The cross section of a leaf is shown in Fig. 3.2.

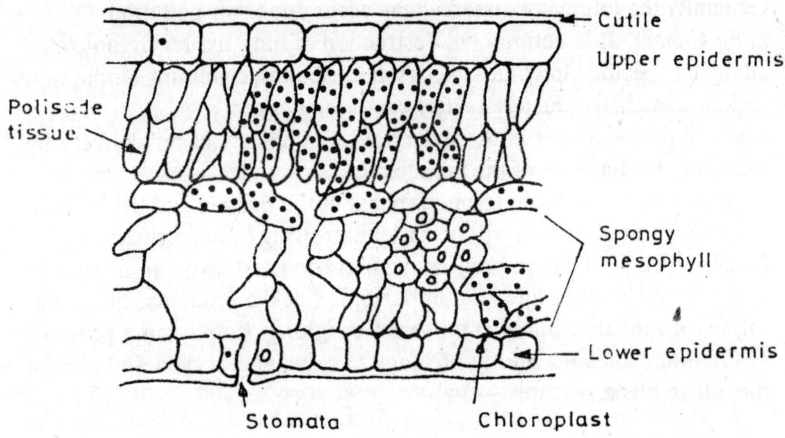

Fig. 3.2.

The damage caused by air pollutants may be classified as follows.

(a) Necrosis
(b) Chlorosis
(c) Epinasty
(d) Leaf abscission
(e) Acute injury
(f) Chronic injury

Necrosis: Necrosis is the killing of tissues or destruction of leaf tissues or severe drying.

Chlorosis: Chlorosis is the loss or reduction of chlorophyll which results disappearance of green colour.

Epinasty: Epinasty is a downward curvature of the leaf due to high rate of growth on the upper surface.

Leaf Abscission: Leaf abscission is the dropping of leaves .

Acute Injury: Acute injury is the severe visible damage to leaf tissues. It results due to short time exposure of pollutants of relatively high concentrations.

Chronic Injury: Chronic injury is the injury due to long term exposure of pollutants of low concentrations.

Ozone: Citrus growth is inhibited by the ozone. Reddish-brown pigmentation appears on the upper surfaces of tomatoes by the ozone. Mostly ozone attacks on the palisade region in the mesophyll.

PAN: Peroxy actyl nitrate attacks the spongy parenchyma cells surrounding the air space and cause silvering or bronzing of the lower leaf area. At 0.01 ppm for 6-h exposure damage the vegetation.

SO_2: Sulphurdioxide enters the stomata directly and the plants cells in the mesophyll. It converts to sulphite and later to sulphate. Cotton and barley are effected at 0.3 to 0.5 ppm for 8-h exposure.

CO: Carbon monoxide has no detrimental effect on vegetation.

Hydrogen Fluoride: Hydrogen fluoride causes the burning of tip and margin of leaves of plants. Grapes are sensitive to fluorides and the damage is significant even at 1 ppb concentrations.

Ethylene: Ethylene causes epinasty and leaf abscission. It causes plant damage at ambient levels of 0.001 to 0.005 ppm. 0.05 ppm for 6-h exposure is the threshold concentration.

NO_2: NO_2 causes supressed growth in beans and tomatoes.

The damage of specific air pollutants to vegetation is shown in Table 3.2(a).

Table 3.2(a). Damage of specific air pollutants to vegetation

Pollutant ppm	Concentration time, h	Exposure	Symptoms
Sulphur dioxide	0.03	8	Bleached spots and areas chlorosis, growth reduction
Ozone	0.03	4	Bleaching and growth reduction growth supression
PAN	0.01	6	Glazing, Silvering, bronzing on lower surface of leaves
Chlorine	0.10	2	Bleaching between veins, tip, and leaf abscission
Ethylene	0.05	6	Flower dropping, withering, leaf abnormalities
Hydrogen fluoride	0.0001	5 weeks	Tip and margin burn, yield reduction, chlorosis

3.4. EFFECTS ON MATERIALS AND PROPERTY

Air pollution causes damage on materials and property which is termed as "economic loss". The damage is mostly on exposed constructional materials like stones, bricks, metals, mortar, wood, paints, electric wirings, and also on rubber, paper, leather and textile materials. These materials may be damaged by the process of (i) abrasion, (ii) chemical attack either directly or indirectly, (iii) deposition, (iv) corrosion, and (v) any combination of above.

(i) *Abrasion:* Travelling of particulate matter in air with higher velocities cause abrasive action on the obstruction materials. This is due to physical action.

(ii) *Chemical Attack:* Pollutants reacts with the material surfaces and make them deteriorate. Some of them may react directly. e.g.: bleaching of marble by sulphur dioxide, tarnishing of silver.
Indirect action means that certain materials absorb pollutants and undergo some chemical reactions. The product of the reaction damage the material. e.g.: absorption of sulphurdioxide by leather. In the presence of moisture, SO_2 in leather produce sulphuric acid, which deteriorates the leather.

(iii) *Deposition:* Particulate matter deposit on the materials and their aesthetic appearance may be reduced.

(iv) *Corrosion:* Deposition of pollutants on the moistured metal surfaces destroys the protective film of oxygen by electrochemical process. Wind velocity, temperature, moisture, and sunlight will influence the rate of damage.

Damage of air pollution to various materials are shown in Table 3.2(b). Sulphur compounds are responsible for the major damage to materials. SO_2 is the most detrimental pollutants that contributes to metal corrosion. Aluminium is fairly resistant to SO_2 attack. When humidity is more than 70%, corrosion rate is greatly increased. Hydrocarbons cause no appreciable corrosive damage to materials. Carbon monoxide appears to have no detrimental effect on material surfaces. Paints drying is inhibited by 1 to 2 ppm of sulphurdioxide and paint is blacked by hydrogen sulphide. At 2 ppm, sulphurdioxide causes embrittlement of paper. Textiles of nylon especially nylon hose strength is weakened by sulphurdioxide or sulphuric acid mist aerosol.

3.5. REDUCTION OF VISIBILITY

American Meteorology Society (Boston), defined the visibility as "the greatest distance in a given direction at which it is just possible to see and identify with the unaided eye, (a) in a day time, a prominent dark object against the sky at the horizon and (b) at night, a known preferably unfocussed moderately intense light source.

Table 3.2(b). Effects of air pollution on materials

Material	Effects	Pollutant	Action
Building material	(1) Physical erosion (2) Oily look (3) Discolouration $CaSO_4$ stains on the building surfaces	(1) Particulates (2) Oily matter (3) SO_2	(1) Abrasive action (2) Embedding in building surfaces (3) Lime stone, marble contain $CaCO_3$ & $MgCO_3$ $CaCO_3 + SO_2 \longrightarrow CaSO_4$ Presence of SO_2 in moist atmosphere form H_2SO_4. This reacts with $CaCO_3$.
Metals	Corrosion and spoilage of surface	SO_2 acid gases	Sulphur oxides in the air reacts with metals and corrode more rapidly
Paints	Defading of surfaces and discolouration	SO_2, H_2S	Paint containing lead pigments reacts with H_2S ; $Pb + H_2S \longrightarrow PbS$
Rubber	Cracking of rubber and weakening	Ozone & oxidants	Weathering and oxidizing of ozone
Paper	White turns yellow (discolouration) and Embrittlement	SO_2	Electrochemical deterioration paper tends to react with SO_2 gives H_2SO_4.
Leather	Leather becomes brittle and cause its deterioration	SO_2	Readily absorption of SO_2 by leather and react with moisture in leather tends to form H_2SO_4
Textiles	Tensile strength, wear life reduced, and spotting.	Particulates	Abrasive action
	Deterioration of natural and synthetic fibers.	SO_2	Chemical action
Textile dyes	Fading (yellowing of white fabrics)	NO_x, O_3 (high level of NO_2)	Chemical action
Ceramics & Glass	Change in surface apperance.	Hydrogen Fluoride & acid gases	Pollutants react with silicon compounds

Visibility is the maximum distance possible to see and identify with an unaided eye in a given direction. The visibility is reduced by scatter of sun light by particulates and is more when relative humidity is less than 70%. Presence of submicron particles in the atmosphere with concentration of 150 micrograms of cubic meter can reduce visibility of 3.5 km. Hygroscopic particulates (particles that collect water from the atmosphere and form, a mist), carbon, tar, metal particles in the atmosphere also reduce visibility. Crystalline compounds like iron, aluminium, silicon, and calcium associate with sulphates, nitrates, chlorides, and fluorides also reduce visibility.

Particulate concentrations of 100,000/cm^3 can reduce visibility to 1.6 km. NO_2 at 0.25 ppm. will cause reduction of visibility and at 8 to 10 ppm., it reduces visibility up to 1.6 km. NO_2 absorbs light and causes the sky to appear brownish in colour. Visibility is greatly effected by concentrations of Sulphur dioxide more than 100 micrograms/m^3 and particles in the size range of 0.1 to 1.0 microns particulates and SO_2 of 150 micrograms/m^3 with relative humidity of less than 70% can reduce visibility upto 8 km. Concentration of 0.1 ppm of SO_2 with a significant concentration of particulate matter and relative humidity of 50% can also reduce visibility to about 8 km. Solid and liquid particles in the submicron range from 0.1 to 1.0 micron are responsible for the decrease in visibility. Particulate concentration of 750 μg/m^3 accompanied by 715 μg/m^3 of sulphurdioxide of 24-h average can increases the illness. Children likely to experience increased incidence of respiratory diseases for concentration of 120 μg/m^3 of particulate matter and sulphurdioxide with annual mean concentration.

To determine the visibility the following formula may be adopted.

$$V = 5.2\ T\ r\ /\ (K \cdot C) \qquad (3.1)$$

where

V = visibility, km

T = density of particles, kg/m^3

r = radius of particles, micrometers

K = scattering area ratio, dimensionless

C = concentration of particles, micrograms per m^3

This is not valid when the humidity is greater than 70%.

SHORT/FILL UP THE BLANK TYPE QUESTIONS

Effects on Plants and Animals

1. *Cement* dust plug leaf stomata and block light for photosynthesis.
2. *Lime* deposits on plant leaves which cause reduction in plant photosynthesis.
3. Sensitive plants for air pollution are *tobacco, raddish, potato,* and *tomato.*
4. Resistant plants for air pollution are *bean, strawberry and carrot.*
5. *Ethylene* effects the dropping of flowers of the plants and failure of leaf to open properly.
6. *Hydrogen fluoride* earliest effect on vegetation is the tip and margin burning.
7. *Fluorides* when exposed to extremely low concentrations, plants will eventually accumulate enough to injure the leaf tissue.
8. Fluorine as gaseous hydrogen fluoride and silicon tetrafluoride concentrations of the order of *1 ppb* can be significant to plant damage.
9. Grapes pines and large seed fruits are quite sensitive to *fluorides.*
10. Accumulation of *solid* fluorides on a leaf surface will not injure the leaf.
11. In grasses the tips become brown coloured after exposure to low concentrations of *hydrogen chlorides.*

12. Light spots on tobacco leaves is partly due to *ozone.*
13. *Ozone* hits on tomato, tobacco, potato and corn leaves tend to collapse.
14. *Selenium* in small amounts is required for the growth of some plants, which accumulate high concentrations thereby become poisonous to animals to eat them.
15. *CO* is non-toxic to insects and other lower forms of life which have no red blood cells.
16. Many green plants are sensitive to *sulphurdioxide* and are injured by exposure of a few hours to conentrations as low as 0.3 ppm.
17. Injury by ozone is identified by *stippling or flecking* on the leaves.
18. Injury by PAN is identified by *bronzing, glazing,* and *silvering* on the under surface of the leaves.
19. The major toxic gas pollutant of air that causes vegetation injury is hydrogen fluoride.
20. *Asparages, cotton, pear, strawberry and tomato* plants collect remarkable concentration of fluorine upto several hundred ppm without showing any signs of damage.
21. *Fluorides* cause softened bones, anemia and loss of weight.
22. Hay fever is caused due to aero allergens (plant pollen)in the atmosphere.
23. Destruction of leaf tissues, severe drying or burning of leaves of plants due to air pollution is called *necrosis.*
24. *Arsenic* cause depressed nervous system, loss of appetite, loss of weight and paralysis of animals.
25. *Ragweed plants pollen* causes Hay fever.

Effects on Human Health and Materials

26. Inhalation of cotton fibre dust over long periods of time gives chronic cough called *byssinosis.*
27. *Emphysema* is a progressive breakdown of air sacs in the lungs usually brought about by chronic infection of the bronchial tubes. This disease progressively diminishes the ability of the lungs to transfer oxygen to the blood stream and carbondioxide from it.
28. *Bronchitis* (asthma) is a disease in which trachea and bronchi show an increased responsiveness to various stimuli, as manifested by a widespread narrowing of the air ways.
29. One of the most common effects of air pollution is the reduction in *visibility.*
30. Reduction in visibility by air pollution occurs due to *absorption and scattering* of light by air borne liquid and solid materials.
31. Exposure of high levels of *NO_x and ozone* and high humidity can cause fading of textile dyes, yellowing of white fabric and oxidation of metals.
32. *400 to 500 ppm* of sulphurdioxide exposure for a short period is dangerous to health.
33. *Smog* causes irritation of nose and throat, watering of the eyes, diminishes visibility.
34. Beryllium oxide dust causes *berrylliosis* of the lungs.
35. *Beryllium* causes reduction in body resistance to respiratory diseases like *pneumonia and emphysema.*
36. Cancer of the lips and ,mouth are due to exposure of *beryllium oxide.*
37. *Inorganic lead* causes liver, kidney damage mental health effects in children and abnormalities in fertility and pregnancy.
38. *750 ppm of CO* may cause death after a short continuous exposure period.
39. *Ozone* attacks synthetic rubbers, there by reducing the life of tyres and insulation.
40. *Ozone* attacks the cellulose in textiles.

41. Oxidants primarily PAN and PBN cause severe eye irritation and in combination with ozone, they irritate *nose and throat.*
42. Unvolcanised rubber strips are hung inside the shelter to determine rubber cracking effects of *Ozone* in the atmosphere.
43. Dyed *cotton fabric* panels are used to determine fading of dyes due to chemicals in the atmosphere.
44. Reduction in sharpness of vision is due to excess *CO.*
45. Upper respiratory tract removes particulates larger than *10 microns* in diameter.
46. Particles less than *2* microns in diameter may enter the deepest areas of the lungs.
47. *CO* is an asphyxiating gas in enclosed places like tunnels.
48. *CO* in ambient atmosphere may cause headaches, loss of visual acuity, loss of ability to accurately estimate time intervals, decreased muscular coordination and loss of oxygen from the blood.
49. *Oxides of nitrogen* cause lung tissues to becomes leathery and brittle and may cause lung cancer and emphysema.
50. Buildings are affected by the abrasive action of particulate pollutants cause *physical erosion.*
51. Building stones such as lime stones, sand stone of marble are affected by air pollutants like *sulphurdioxide.*
52. Paints containing lead pigments darken through the formation of lead sulphide when *hydrogen sulphide* is present as a pollutant of concentration of 0.1 ppm within 1-h.
53. A white house turns a dirty gray and other colours due fade when H_2S present in air.
54. Paper exposed to *sulphurdioxide* in the atmosphere turns yellow and brittle.
55. *Chromium* in the form of chromic acid also turns paper brittle and yellow.
56. SO_x *and other acid aerosols* in the atmosphere cause increased runs in nylons stockings and loss in strength in cotton curtains.
57. NO_x, SO_2, *and ozone* cause dyes to fade and white fabrics to turn yellow.
58. Nasal hairs remove particles of size greater than *10* microns
59. The maximum size of particles that can be inhaled into the lungs is *5 microns* in diameter.
60. *Carbondioxide and methane* can cause death by causing a deficiency of oxygen that destroy brain cells and damages the central nervous system.
61. *Antimony* from metal oxides causes irreversible damage to the heart and also the kidneys by inflicting tubular cells damage.
62. *Arsenic* causes stomach and intestinal problems.
63. *Asbestosis* is the fibrous magnesium silicate minerals.
64. *Cadmium* causes lung damage by chest pain, breathlessness, seating.
65. Exposure to metallic *mercury* vapour may cause injury to the central nervous system and kidneys.
66. *Fluorides* causes mottled teeth, softened bones anemia and loss of weight of animals.
67. Exposure of *hydrogen sulphide* leads to eye irritation, conjunctivitis and visual impairment.
68. *Hydrogen sulphide* is an irritating and asphyxiating chemical that reacts with the tissues of the body, retards central nervous system and causes headaches and diarrhoea.
69. *Nitrogen oxides* irritate the nose, eyes and lungs.
70. *Oxidants like ozone* causes premature aging increases calcification of bones, reduces body fat and affects vision.
71. *Tobacco smoke* contains many pollutants like CO, CO_2, fly-ash, mineral dust, NO_2, nicotine, formaldehyde.
72. *Fluorides and radio-active* pollutants concentrated through bio-magnification in the

forage can produce increased damage to the animals and their milk product.

73. Particles in the size range 0.38 to 0.76 μm and gas molecules of sulphurdioxide contribute to reduce *visibility*.
74. Pollutants absorbs and scatter light which reduces visibility by decreasing the contrast between the *object and back ground sky*.
75. Leather upholstery and book bindings become brittle due to absorption of *sulphur dioxide*.
76. Approximately 40% of the particles between *2 - 10 μm* and *2 μm* in size are retained in the bronchioles and olveoli.
77. *CO* reacts with the haemoglobin of blood to give carboxy-haemoglobin.
78. *Hydrogen sulphide* is an extremely compound and readily oxidizes paints and rubber.
79. CO has *200* times more affinity for haemoglobin than oxygen.
80. H_2S erodes the cornea of the eye causing the disorder Kerato conjuctivitis.
81. *Ozone* impairs vision and lowers body temperature.
82. Smog is said to be the cause for *reduction of visibility* effect in many industrial areas.
83. Accumulation of air borne contaminants by forage may cause its effects on *animals*.
84. A blue line along the gums is formed mainly because of *mercury poisoning*.
85. *Rubber* becomes weak and brittle when continuously exposed to ozone-organic oxidants.
86. *Sulphurdioxide* gas causes embrittlement of paper and reduction in tensile strength of textiles.
87. Because of excess *CO* content in blood, one cannot discriminate the "time interval" or the "intensity of brightness ".
88. *Sulphurdioxide* gas induces bronchitis and pulmonary emphysema.
89. Asbestosis is a magnesium silicate causing difficult breathing, coughing and lung cancer.
90. *500 ppm* of NO_2 may induce death.
91. Defading of colour by sulphurdioxide can be reduced by using *zinc and titanium* based paints.
92. Concentrations of hydrogen fluoride even in ppb level being capable of causing visible damage to plants like gladiolus and pines.
93. Hydrogen sulphide differ from many other toxic gases, which scorches growing leaves instead of attacking mature, older leaves.
94. Symptoms of nitrogendioxide injury appears as irregular white or brown collapsed lessions on tissues between veins and near the leaf margin.
95. Yellow-green mottling and stipping of cotton leaves is due to damage of PAN, oxidant.
96. Selenium is required for growth of plants which may accumulate high concentrations of selenium, there by become poisonous to animals by eating that vegetation.
97. Accumulation of selenium on plants like wheat, barley, even on small amounts.
98. Pumpkins, apples, tomatoes are sensitive to sulphurdioxide a primary pollutant.
99. Smartweed and ragweed are used as sulphurdioxide damage indicators.

CHAPTER 4

Air Sampling and Analysis

4.1 INTRODUCTION

To know the quantitative and qualitative aspects of air pollution, it is necessary to collect the air and analyse for required parameters. A small (relatively) volumes of air are collected and analysed as per the prescribed methods, which is called as sampling and analysis of air.

The sampling of air is broadly classified into two types:

(i) Ambient or atmospheric air sampling, and

(ii) Stack gas sampling.

Whatever the method and purpose of sampling may be the procedure should satisfy the following requirements.

(a) The sample should be representative.

(b) The sample should be preserved properly and analysed as quickly as possible and

(c) The analysed data should be interpreted appropriately.

4.2 FACTORS TO BE CONSIDERED IN SAMPLING

The important factors to be considered in sampling are as follows:

(i) Selection of sampling procedures including procedures of analysis of pollutants.

(ii) Location of sampling stations and

(iii) Period of sampling, etc.

The selection of sampling procedure depends on the type of pollutant to be sampled, method of collection and analysis. A volume of air is collected and analysed for the quantity of pollutant present in the air. The pollutant concentration is expressed in micrograms per cubic meter of air. The location of sampling station and equipment, and sampling period will decide the concentration of pollutant. The volume of sampled air should be large enough for analysis. Peak periods of pollution should be identified and sampling should be done frequently. Generally 8-h sampling period for average values and 1-h or 2-h sampling period for peak value is practised. To obtain average values, sampling should be done at least on cycle of operation (covering both pre-monsoon and post-monsoon). Micrometeorological variations should also be considered while sampling. Some more details are given in Chapter 10.

4.3 AMBIENT OR ATMOSPHERIC AIR SAMPLING

Ambient or atmospheric air sampling means that the sampling of air is collected at free atmosphere, which is done for both particulates and gaseous pollutants.

4.3.1 Objectives of Ambient Air Sampling

The objectives of ambient air sampling are as follows.

(i) To assess the damage caused by the air pollutants to human health, animal and plant life and also to the property.
(ii) To find the level of pollution in different zones like industrial, residential, etc.
(iii) To determine the degree of pollution control required for existing industries.
(iv) To collect the data for formulating and testing the air pollution dispersion models.
(v) To prescribe air quality standards for a city.
(vi) To identify and control traffic pollution, and
(vii) To carry out the research in air pollution monitoring control programmes.

4.3.2 Location of Sampling Station

The location of sampling station should be such that it should be in the free atmosphere, without interferences from stagnant spaces or large buildings, etc. It should be located at a height of minimum 1.5 m but not exceeding 15 m from the ground level. Public buildings like municipal and government offices, school, hospitals etc. are generally preferred for sampling stations. The number of sampling stations, period and rate of sampling is depended upon the requirements of the survey. The following values have been recommended in India:

Period of sampling, h	Rate of sampling, lpm
0.5	2
1.0	1
1.0–4.0	0.5
8.0	0.2
8.0–24	0.1–0.2

Generally the principle involved in sampling of gaseous pollutants is that the gaseous pollutants in air are made to react with liquid absorbing reagents at atmospheric temperature and pressure, when air is bubbled through the absorbing solution in the impinger (also known as bubbler).

The equipment required for carry out the sampling of gaseous air pollutants consists of a standard impinger of 35 ml capacity, a trap (filter either a glass wool or membrane) manometer, a flow meter (a rotameter or a total air gasometer of flow rate ranging from 0.0 to 3.0 lpm), and a suction pump of capacity 5 to 10 lpm with 500 mm Hg vacuum capability and fitted with moisture trap). These are arranged in sequence called as sampling train, which is shown in Fig. 4.1.

4.3.3 Sampling Methods for Particulate Pollutants

The selection of equipment or method for sampling of particulate pollutants is based on the size of particulates to be sampled. If the size is greater than 10 microns, sedimentation based method may be adopted and the size is less than 10 microns, filtration based method etc. may be used.

1. Dust Fall Collector

It is used generally for particles greater than 10 microns to estimate particulate pollutant concentration in air. This equipment is inexpensive and simple to operate. It consists of a plastic or metal jar of about 200 to 300 mm height and 100 to 150 mm in diameter at the base with a tapered of wall from top to bottom. Water is poured upto 100 to 250 mm height, so that insoluble dust reaches and retains at the bottom of the jar. To avoid algal growth in the jar, an algicide (1 mg of of copper sulphate per litre of water) is added to water. During winter, isopropyl

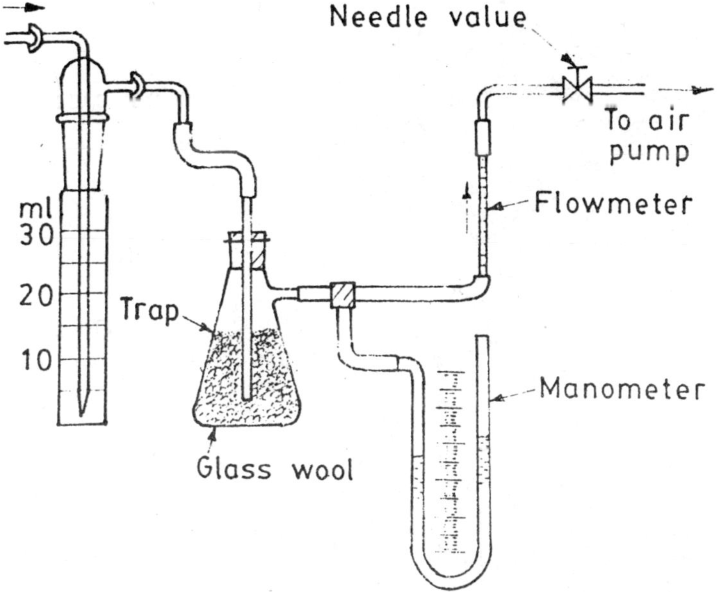

Fig. 4.1. Sampling Train

alcohol may be added as antifreegent to prevent the formation of ice in the jar. This equipment is kept at the required location for a period of 30 days. Just after that, dust is separated from the jar, evaporated and weighed in milligrams. The dust fall rate is expressed in milligrams per square centimeter per 30 days (mg/cm ^{2}/month or tons/ km^2 /month). Even though the equipment is inexpensive and simple to operate, the values are not accurate and not reproducible. Hence they can be used to measure the relative pollution level or trends in an area over a period of time.

2. *High Volume Air Sampler*

The high volume air sampler is a popular and frequently used equipment for the determination of suspended particulate matter (SPM) in air. The principle involved in this method is that the particles are filtered from known volume of an air sample by a suction apparatus (a vacuum pump) and the particles are made to deposit on a porous filter paper. The commonly used high volume sample ('Micrometal' make, Bombay and other similar makes).

The high volume air sampler consists of the following, as shown in Fig. 4.2.

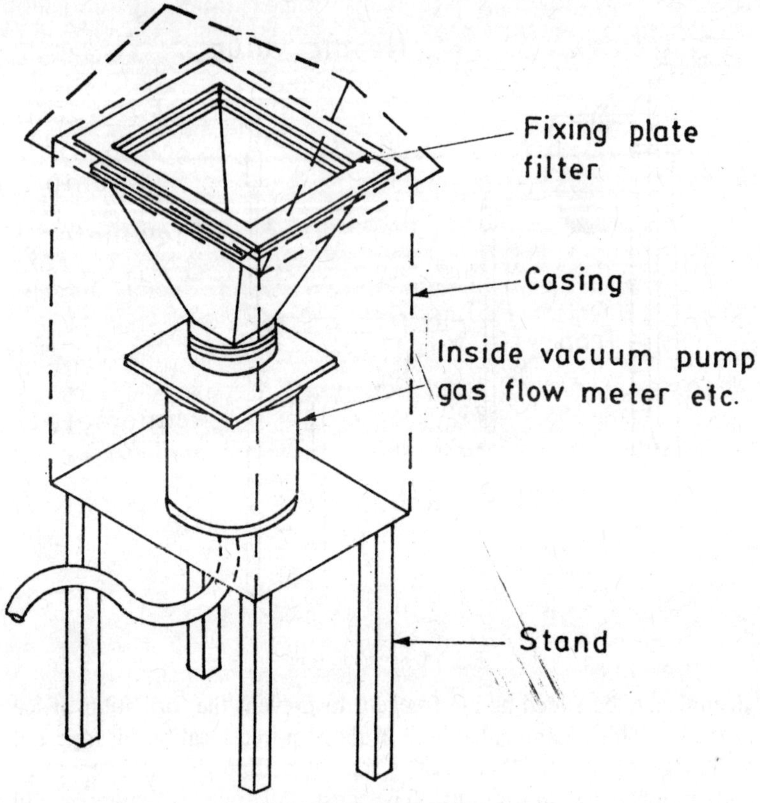

Fig. 4.2. Assembled Sampler and Shelter

(a) face plate and gasket
(b) filter paper (preferably whatman make), and fitting assembly
(c) vacuum pump (air sucker) with air flow measuring device and
(d) casing with a roof

The filter plate provides the base for sitting the filter paper of size 200 mm × 250 mm, through which air sample is collected by creating suction in the filter area. This suction is created by a vacuum pump with a flow rate of 25 lpm. These conditions will permit the sampling of abient air for a period of 8-h. The suspended particles of size less than 10 microns and greater than 3 microns are retained on the filter. The duration of sampling is measured in an elapsed time meter which is placed in series with the blower. A rotameter or a manometer is provided to measure the volume of air passed through the filter. Generally 'Whatman make' filter papers are widely used. The concentration of the pollutants is expressed as micrograms per cubic meter which is calculated from the observed data as given below.

Calculation of the result:

$$C = \frac{W_t - W_I}{V} \times 10^6$$

where

C = Concentration of suspended particulate matter (SPM) in micrograms per cubic meter

W_I = Weight of filter paper before sampling, or Initial mass of filter, g

W_t = Weight of filter paper after sampling, g (keep the filter paper in a desiccator for 24-h after sampling)

V = Volume of air sampled in cubic meter at STP

$= \frac{(Q_I + Q_t)}{2} \times t$

Q_I = Air flow rate through clean filter (initial flow rate, cubic meter per minute)

Q_t = Air flow rate at the end of the sampling, cubic meter per minute

t = Sampling period, minutes

For details refer IS: 5182 (part IV) - 1973, code of Indian Standard for measurement of air pollution.

Model calculation:

Example: Air flow rate at the beginning of sampling is 2 m^3/min. and air flow rate at the end of sampling is 1.5 m^3/min. Sampling period is 24-h and weight of the clean filter is 3.5 g and weight of the filter after sampling is 4.0 g average temperature is 30 °C and average pressure at the sample location is 715 mm of Hg.

Solution:

Average air flow rate = (2.0 + 1.5) / 2 = 1.75 m^3/min

Volume of air sampled = 1.75 × 24 × 60 = 2520 m^3

Correction for temperature and pressure:

$$PV/T = P_1V_1/T_1$$

$$760\ V/273 = 715 \times 2520/303$$

$$V = 2136\ m^3$$

Weight of particulate matter = $W_t - W_I$ = 4.0–3.5 = 0.5 g

SPM (micrograms per cubic meter) = Weight of particulate matter, in micrograms/Volume of air sampled, cubic meter. SPM (micrograms per cubic meter) = $0.5 \times 10^6/2136$ = 234

3. *Other Methods*

To collect the particulate matter from air, samplers like paper tape air samplers, Durham sampler, Andersom sampler, Greenlarg-impinger and cyclone sampler are used. The principle involved in these methods is based on inertial impingment. In this technique, an obstacle is placed against the polluted air flow to change the direction of flow, but the particles continue to travel in the inertial direction. When the particles hit the obstacle, there they attach to the adhesive surface of the obstacle. The particles are separated by immersing the obstacle in a liquid (scrubber).

4.3.4 Sampling Methods of Gaseous Pollutants

The sampling methods of gaseous pollutants are classified into three types which are as follows.

(i) Absorption
(ii) Adsorption, and
(iii) Condensation

(i) Absorption

In this method, a gaseous pollutant in air is removed by providing through contact with a chemical which can absorb the pollutant in a closed container under specific conditions and a new substance is formed. After sampling, the gaseous pollutant is estimated based on any convenient characteristic of newly formed substance (e.g.: colour). The results are expressed into micrograms per cubic meter. This method can be used for sampling sulphurdioxide, oxides of nitrogen, hydrogen sulphide, ammonia and aldehydes in air using absorbing reagents for each gas.

(ii) Adsorption

In this method, gaseous pollutant are made to attract to the surfaces of a solid media (adsorbent) and retained there. The efficiency of the system mostly depended on the surface area of the adsorbent surface and several other factors. By this method, ammonia, oxides of nitrogen carbonmonoxide, hydrogen sulphide and sulphurdioxide etc. may be sampled.

There are some advantages using adsorption instead of absorption in the sampling of gaseous pollutants.

(a) Due to colour formation, pollutant are easily identified.
(b) The sample can be easily transported because pollutant is retained in solid media.

(c) Highly volatile gases with high concentrations are also completed collected.

(iii) Condensation

This method is used for sampling of hydrocarbons, radioactive gases etc. The gas is sucked through collection chambers (sampling train) in which temperature is progressively lowered. If the temperature in the collection chamber is equal to the boiling temperature, the gas turns to liquid and condensate. Sampling trains with freezing facility enables to collect several gases at the same period.

4.4 STACK GAS SAMPLING

4.4.1 Introduction

Stack gas sampling or source sampling means that the sampling is done at the source (origin) of pollutants, where they enter into the atmosphere. Generally stacks are used to discharge the pollutants into the atmosphere, hence the sampling is done in the stacks at a specified height (prescribed) from ground level.

The objectives of the stack sampling are as follows.

(i) To determine the quantity and the type of pollutants emitted from a specified source.

(ii) To determine the efficiency of a pollutant control device.

(iii) To monitor the emission standards so that the review may be made on the air quality management programme.

4.4.2 Stack Sampling Procedure

The stack sampling procedure consists of the following components.

(i) Selection of sampling position in the stack

(ii) Measurement of gas flow rate

(iii) Measurement of velocity of gas in the stack, and

(iv) Determination of temperature of gas.

(i) Selection of sampling position in the stack

The sample to be collected from a stack should be a representative sample (it should represent the true composition and characteristics of the polluted gas coming out of the stack). In practice, representative sample is obtained by averaging the number of samples taken in a correct location. The location of sample should be such that it should not get disturbances by bends, baffles, etc. It is preferably at straight portion of the stack. A typical location is shown in Fig. 4.3.

To get average concentration, samples are collected at various points across the stack. The temperature and velocity of gas varies from point to point within the diameter of the stack, which will change the pollutant concentrations. For rectangular stacks, the equivalent diameter is calculated from the following equation.

Equivalent diameter = 2 (Length × Width)/(Length + Width).

A typical cross-section layout and location of traverse points for circular and rectangular stacks are given in Fig. 4.4 and Table 4.1.

The minimum number of traverse points is four and there after additives of four, as given below.

Cross-sectional area of stack square meters	Number of points
0.2	4
> 0.2 to 2.5	12
> 2.5	20

(ii) Measurement of gas flow rate (pollutant emission rate)

The gas flow rate through the stack is determines by the continuity equation, which are as follows.

$$Q = U_s \times A \tag{4.1}$$

where

Q = Average volumetric gas flow rate, litres per minute

U_s = Average stack gas velocity, m/s

A = Cross-sectional area of the stack, m^2

(iii) Measurement of Stack Gas Velocity

Stack gas velocity is determined by a pitot-tube in combination with a double differential manometer, which is shown in Fig. 4.5

A double pitot-tube which consists of two openings having faces (entrances) opposite to each other. This arangement is connected to the incline manometer. The velocity head is estimated from the deflections in the manometer with a known coefficient. The velocity

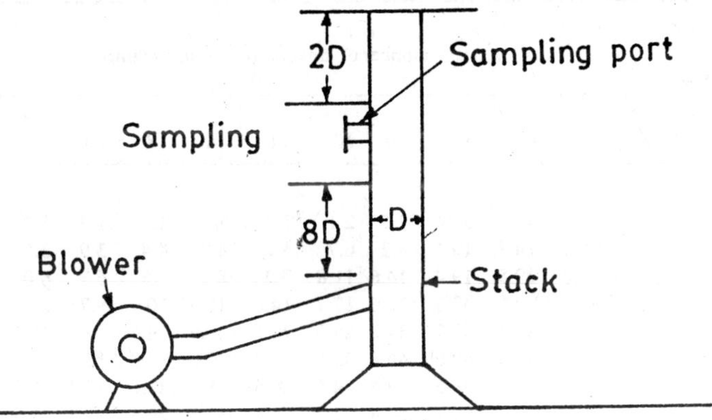
2D
Sampling port
Sampling
8D
D
Blower
Stack

Fig. 4.3.

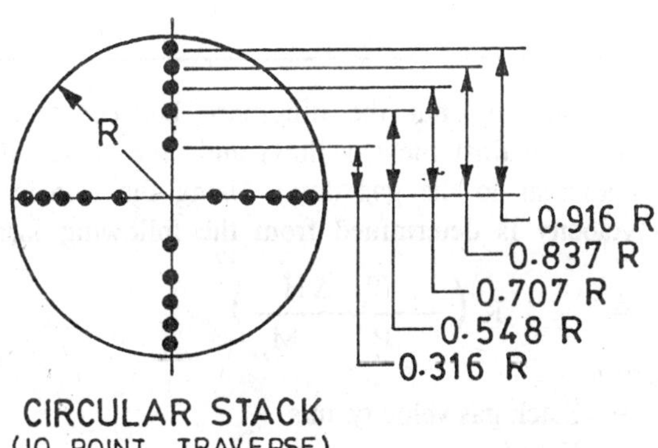
RECTANGULAR STACK
(MEASURE AT CENTER OF AT LEAST 9 EQUAL AREAS)
R
0.916 R
0.837 R
0.707 R
0.548 R
0.316 R
CIRCULAR STACK
(10 POINT TRAVERSE)

Fig. 4.4.

Table 4.1. Location of Traverse Points in Circular Stacks.

Traverse point number on a diameter	number of traverse points on a diameter										
	4	6	8	10	12	14	16	18	20	22	24
1	6.7	4.4	3.3	2.5	2.1	1.8	1.6	1.4	1.3	1.2	1.1
2	25.0	14.7	10.5	8.2	6.7	5.7	4.9	4.4	3.9	3.5	3.2
3	75.0	29.5	19.4	14.6	11.8	9.9	8.5	7.5	6.7	6.0	5.5
4	93.3	70.5	32.3	22.6	17.7	14.6	12.5	10.9	9.7	8.7	7.9
5		85.3	67.7	34.2	25.0	20.1	16.9	14.6	12.9	11.6	10.5
6		95.6	80.6	65.8	35.5	26.9	22.0	18.8	16.5	14.6	13.2
7			89.5	77.4	64.5	36.6	28.3	23.6	20.4	18.0	16.1
8			96.7	85.4	75.0	63.4	37.5	29.6	25.0	21.8	19.4
9				91.8	82.3	73.1	62.5	38.2	30.6	26.1	23.0
10				97.5	88.2	79.9	71.7	61.8	38.8	31.5	27.2
11					93.3	85.4	78.0	70.4	61.2	39.3	32.3
12					97.9	90.1	83.1	76.4	69.4	60.7	39.8
13						94.3	87.5	81.2	75.0	68.5	60.2
14						98.2	91.5	85.4	79.6	73.9	67.7
15							95.1	89.1	83.5	78.2	72.8
16							98.4	92.5	87.1	82.0	77.0
17								95.6	90.3	85.4	80.6
18								98.6	93.3	88.4	83.9
19									96.1	91.3	86.8
20									98.7	94.0	89.5
21										96.5	92.1
22										98.9	94.5
23											96.8
24											98.9

head is nothing but the difference between the impact pressure (measured against the gas flow) and the static pressure (measured perpendicular to the gas flow). Using the velocity head, the stack gas velocity is determined from the following formula:

$$U_s = K\left(\frac{T_s \ \Delta H}{P_s \ M_s}\right)^{1/2} \quad (4.2)$$

where

U_s = Stack gas velocity, m/s
K = $K_p \times C_p$
K_p = Dimension constant, = 33.5
C_p = Pitot-tube coefficient, (0.96)
T = Temperature of stack gas. °K

ΔH = Velocity head, mm of water
P_a = Absolute pressure of the stack gas,.mm Hg
M_s = Molecular weight of stack gas

Isokinetic Conditions in Sampling

To get a representative sample, sampling should be done under isokinetic condition which means, that the velocity of the stack gas stream entering the probe nozzle must be same as the velocity of the stream passing the nozzle.

If the sampling velocity is very high, a convergent stream will develop at the nozzle face which causes entry of more lighter particles into the probe. Particles of size greater than 3 microns may travel along the edge of nozzle and escape from the sampling. Then sampling will be erroneous and will not be representative. If the sampling velocity (velocity in the probe) is less than the velocity of stack gas flow, a divergent air stream will develop at the nozzle face with high deflected velocity. The lighter particles which may pass on along deflected gas stream and will not be collected by the probe. Due to inersia, heavy particles may enter the probe. This condition will give the sample with high concentration of heavy particles. Hence sampling should be done at isokinetic condition.

(iv) Determination of Temperature of Gas

Generally stack gases contain high temperature because these gases are liberated from the manufacturing processes which involve with high temperature and pressure. Hence, it is necessary to measure temperature of the stack gases to estimate the gas characteristics. The temperature of the gases are measured by using mercury thermometers, thermocouple-pyrometers, etc. Thermocouple censors which consists of probes, measure temperature at all traverse points across the cross-section of the stack. Continuous recording of temperature during the period of sampling is desirable. The probe is selected based on the temperature of the gas and probes used for different temperature ranges are as follows.

Type of probe	Temperature range, °C
Chromel/Alumel	150–1260
Copper/Constantan	150–350
Iron/Constantan	115–1010
Platinum/Platinum	upto 1540

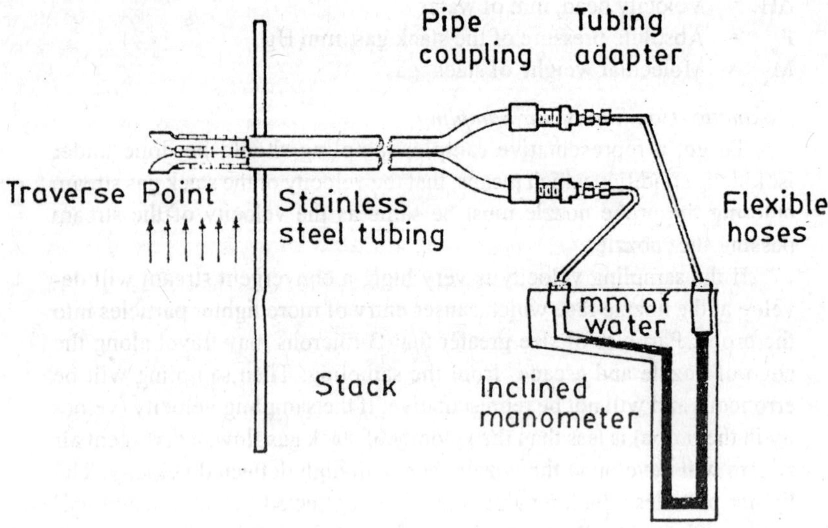

Fig. 4.5. Pitot Tube Manometer Assembly.

4.4.3 Particulate Sampling

To carry out particulate sampling in the stack, sampling train equipment is necessary, which is shown in Fig. 4.6. The sampling train consists of nozzles of various sizes, sampling probe, thimble (filter to retain particulates), gas collector, gas flow meter and a vacuum pump. The procedure for calculating pollutant emission rate is as follows. Before proceeding the stack monitoring, empty thimble weight (W_t) and also inner diameter of the stack, etc. are recorded. The procedure is as follows.

(a) Location of sampling port is fixed as per the requirements or specified by the competent authorities like pollution control board etc. Generally sampling port location is fixed at 7.5 m above ground level.

(b) Shift the stack monitoring equipment to platform which is constructed generally one meter below the sampling port. Record the temperature of the gas by inserting thermo-couple probe at required traverse points.

(c) Insert the pitot tube into the stack and adjust the probe for isokinetic conditions. The manometer and temperature readings are recorded and gas velocity is estimated using the equation 4.2. Gas flow rate is computed by multiplying stack velocity with cross-sectional area of the stack at sampling location.

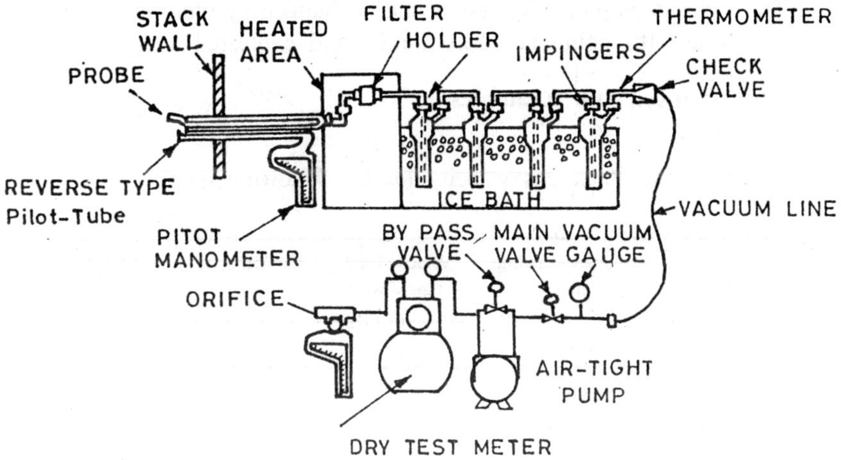

Fig. 4.6.

(d) Insert the sampling train probe at traverse point 1 and start the pump and adjust gas flow till the rotameter reading shows the required (pre-determined) value, say 20 lpm (10-30). Switch-off the pump after sampling is completed in a specified period.

(e) Read the vacuum of the dry gas meter and also the temperature in the gas meter.

The procedure from (a) to (e) is repeated at all the traverse points. Remove the probe from the stack and allow it to cool.

(f) Remove the thimble carefully from the probe and weigh it (W_2). The difference of weight (W_2-W_1) gives the dust collection during the sampling period.

(g) The volume of the gas collected during sampling is obtained by multiplying the rotameter reading or dry gas meter reading (lpm) with sampling period and expressed in cubic meters.

4.4.4 Gaseous Sampling

Gaseous sampling involves the collection of gas from the stack and passing through the absorber or adsorbers or freezers of pollutants, where the gaseous pollutants are removed from the collected gas. A vacuum pump is used to suck the gas from the stack and the volume of gas is recorded by a rotameter. The gas flow rate is expressed as cubic meter per hour. The gaseous pollutants are analysed in the laboratory and are expressed in ppm. or micrograms per cubic meter. The gaseous pollutants emission rate is obtained by multiply the gas flow rate with pollutant concentration and expressed as g/h.

4.5. Worked Out Examples

Calculate the stack gas velocity for the following data

Traverse point	Manometer reading mm	Velocity head mm of water	Gas temp. °C	col.4 + 273 = T_a
col.1	col.2	col.3	col.4	col. 5
1	2.0	1.60	500	773
2	3.8	3.04	520	793
3	5.0	4.00	640	913
4	5.6	4.48	600	873
				avg. 838

The specific gravity of gas is 0.8 and its molecular weight of stack gas is 30. Stack pressure is 770 mm of Hg. Pitot coefficient is 0.96 and K_p is 33.5.

Solution

Typical calculation for traverse point 1.

Stack gas velocity calculation :

U_s = $K (T_s \; \Delta H / P_a \, M_s)^{0.5}$

K = $K_p \times C_p$ = 33.5×0.96 = 32.16

T_s = Temperature of stack gas 500 + 273 = 773 °K

ΔH = Velocity head, mm of water

= Manometer reading × specific gravity of fluid

= $2 \times 0.8 = 1.6$ mm of water

$(T \, \Delta H)^{0.5}$ = $(773 \times 1.6)^{0.5}$ = 35.168

$K/(P_s \, M_s)^{0.5}$ = $32.16/(770 \times 30)^{0.5}$ = 0.2116

Velocity of gas at traverse point 1 = 0.2116×35.168

= 7.44 m/s

Similarly, for traverse points 2, 3, and 4, U_s is calculated and shown in col.8 of the table.

Calculation of particulate matter emission rate:

Diameter of nozzle = 6.5 mm

Vacuum pressure gauge reading = 130 mm

Temperature of the gas = T_m = 37 °C = 37 + 273 = 310 °K

Cross-section area of nozzle = 3.14 d.d/4 = 0.3318 sq.cm

Discharge rate = 7.441 × 0.3318 = 0.0184 cubic meter/min

The flow rate has to be adjusted to dry gas meter condition.

Temperature correction at 1 = T_m/T_s = 310/773 = 0.40104

Pressure correction of first reading 1 = $\dfrac{P_s}{(P_s - P_m)}$

= 770/(770–30) = 770/640 = 1.203125

Sampling rate = 0.0184 × 0.40104 × 1.203125

= 0.00878 cubic meter per minute.

Similarly, for traverse points 2, 3, and 4, sampling flow rate is calculated and are shown in col. 12 of the table.

col.3 × col.5	$\dfrac{K}{(P_s M_s)^{0.5}}$	U_s m/s cols.6 × 7	c.s.area × col.8	$\dfrac{T_s}{T_m}$	$\dfrac{P_s}{P_s - P_m}$	cols.. 9 × 10 × 11
col.6	col.7	col.8	col.9	col.10	col.11	col.12
35.168	0.2116	7.441	0.0184	0.4010	1.2031	0.00878
49.100	0.2116	10.389	0.0206	0.3909	1.2031	0.00969
60.431	0.2116	12.787	0.0254	0.3395	1.2031	0.01037
62.538	0.2116	13.233	0.0263	0.3471	1.2031	0.0109
	avg.	10.962			total	0.03982

The volume of the gas sampled at dry condition = Total of col.12 × samples period (5 min.) = 0.1991 cubic meter.

The volume of the gas samples has to be corrected to STP (i.e.) standard temperature and pressure, at 25 °C and 760 mm of Hg (1 atmosphere).

$$P_1 V_1/T_1 = P_2 V_2/T_2$$

1 stands for standard condition and 2 stands for sampling condition,

Hence, V_1 = Volume of the gas at STP = $(T_1 P_2/T_2 P_1) \times V_2$

= 298 × 640/ (310 × 760) × 0.1991 = 0.1615 m^3

Particulate matter accumulated = $W_2 - W_1$ = 2g.

Particulate loading rate = 2 / 0.16158 = 12.377 g/m^3

Stack cross-sectional area = 3.14 d. d/4

= 3.14 × 0.6 × 0.6/4

= 0.28274 m^2

Discharge rate of stack gas = 0.28274 × 10.962 × 60

Q = 185.966 m^3/min

Q at STP = 762 × 185.966 × 298/(762 × 838)

= 66.131 m^3/min

Particulate matter emission rate = Q × particulate load rate

= 12.377 × 66.131

= 818.55 g/min

= 1.1787 tons/day

4.5 METHOD OF ANALYSIS

The following methods are widely used for the analysis of air pollutants.

(i) Gravimetric methods
(ii) Colourimetry methods
(iii) Absorption of radiation methods, and
(iv) Emission of radiation methods

(i) Gravimetric Methods

In this method the weight of the pollutant is determined (using analytical balance) in a volume of air.

(ii) Colourimetry Methods

This method is popularly used. Inorganic ions like sulphite, nitrite, fluoride, some metal ions and organic compounds are colourless. But they react with certain reagents and produce colour. This colour may be compared with a standard chart or estimated by colourimeter or spectrophotometer, at specified wavelengths.

(iii) Emission of Radiation Methods

In an exited state, any element has its own emission spectrum. The excitement of a pollutant with a flame is measured interms of light emission by photographic methods. This method is popularly used for the estimation of sodium, potassium etc. e.g. flame photometry.

Turbidimetry instruments measure white light transmission when it passes through a finely divided suspension and compares with a standard suspensions.

Nephelometry instruments measure white light reflected from a suspension and compares with a standard suspensions.

Chromatography is method of analysis in which a flow of solvent or a gas initiates the separation of pollutants by differential migration from a narrow initial zone in a adsorptive or absorptive medium. Generally it is used for the analysis of volatile organic compounds.

Gas chromatography is a method of separating the components of a mixture of compounds which are sufficiently volatised to vaporization.

(iv) Absorption of Radiation Methods

These methods enable to identification and quantitative examination of gas in the radiation of gas UV (ultra violet) and IR (infra red) regions. e.g. Atomic absorption spectrophotometer.

4.6 PROCEDURE OF ANALYSIS OF GASEOUS POLLUTANTS IN ATMOSPHERIC AIR

4.6.1 Introduction

The procedure for analysis of sulphurdioxide, sulphation rate, hydrogen sulphide, oxides of nitrogen, oxidants, fluorides, and carbon monoxide are given below. These methods have been adopted by the Bureau of Indian Standards, New Delhi (India), which are given in IS: 5182. (They are reproduced briefly with kind permission of Bureau of Indian standards).

4.6.2 Estimation of Sulphurdioxide from Atmospheric Air

Theory and principles: Even though several methods available for the estimating of sulphurdioxide in air, two methods are popular.

1. Hydrogen peroxide method, which is simple to use and normally operate over periods of 12 to 72 hours. The principle involved in this method is the measurement of acidity increase due to sulphuric acid, which is estimated by titration using an indicator. When air (containing sulphurdioxide) is passed through a dilute hydrogen peroxide at pH 5, then sulphurdioxide in air is absorbed and oxidised to sulphuric acid.
2. Sodium tetra chloromecurate method, which is less simple to operate than hydrogen peroxide method. But, it is suitable for short-term sampling (5 minutes to 6 hours). The principle involved is that, when (air containing sulphurdioxide) is passed through absorber solution of sodium tetra chloromecurate. It forms a stable dichlorosulphito mecurate. If p-rosaniline hydrochloride is added, a colour is produced and the intensity of colour is proportional to the sulphurdioxide present in air. The colour is estimated by using spectrophotometer and the values are reported to the nearest 0.005 ppm at concentration below 0.15 ppm and to the nearest to 0.01 ppm above 1.5 ppm.

If ozone and nitrogendioxide present in air with concentrations more than sulphurdioxide, they interfere in estimation of sulphurdioxide. Hence interferences of nitrogendioxide is eliminated by using 0.06 % sulphamic acid in the absorbing reagent. Heavy metals especially iron salts also interfere in oxidizing dichloro-sulphito mercurate during sample collection. So, interference is eliminated by adding ethylene diamine tetra acetic acid in the absorbing reagent.

Collection of samples: Arrange a sampling train which consists of absorbers, trap to protect flow device, flow control and metering devices, temperature and vacuum gauges, and air pump. They are arranged in the same order. The suction pump and gas meter should be capable of drawing 1.5 lpm. The gas meter should be protected be a moisture trap which contain proper desiccant.

Calibration curve preparation: A calibration curve is prepared by using 0.5, 1.0, 1.5, and 2.0 ml of standard sulphite solution (refer annexure III) into a 100 ml.volumetric flask and dilute to mark with absorbing reagent. The final solution in the flask contains 0.75, 1.5, 2.25, 3.0 microlitres of sulphurdioxide per millilitres. Plot the absorbance (optical density) as the ordinate against the microliters of sulphurdioxide per 10 ml. of absorbance solution on a rectangular co-ordinate paper and draw best fitting straight line.

Procedure: First record the gas meter reading. Pipette exactly 10 ml of absorbing reagent into the absorber. Aspirate the air sample through the absorber at a rate of 0.2 to 2.5 litres per minute. After sampling period (a few minutes to 24 hrs.), the sample contain 2 to 4 microliter of sulphur dioxide in 10 ml of absorbing reagent. Stop the pump and read the final reading of the gas meter.

If necessary, filter the sample to get clarity and make up with distilled water upto 10 ml mark. Add 1.0 ml of p-rosaniline solution and 1.0 ml of the formaldehyde solution and mix well. After 20 minutes, find the absorbance at 560 nm wavelength in a spectrophotometer and read the value from the calibration chart.

Calculation and results: The air is sampled at ambient conditions. Hence, the volume of air is corrected to Standard Temperature and Pressure (STP) conditions, which is as follows.

Based on Boyle's and Charle's law,

$$P_1 \cdot V_1/T_1 \quad = \quad P_2 \cdot V_2/T_2 \qquad (4.3)$$

where P = Pressure; V = Volume and T = Temperature

Suffixes 1 and 2 are the two different conditions.

Similarly, the volume of air at STP (25 °C and 760 mm Hg) is obtained, as follows.

$$V_m = \frac{V(P - P_m)}{760} \times \frac{298}{(T + 273)} \quad (4.4)$$

where

V_m = Volume of air in litres at standard conditions
V = Volume of air in litres at ambient conditions
P = Barometric pressure in mm Hg
P_m = Suction at meter in mm Hg, and
T = Temperature of sampled air in Celsius degrees.

Results: The concentrations of sulphur dioxide in air is calculated as follows.

SO_2, ppm by volume = μl of SO_2/V_m
Where, V_m = Volume of sampled air at STP, and

$$SO_2,\ \mu g/m^3 = \frac{SO_2,\ \text{ppm} \times 64 \times 10^6}{24{,}470} \quad (4.5)$$

4.6.3 Estimation of Sulphation Rate from Atmospheric Air

To determine the average sulphur dioxide concentration for long period over a number of areas in the same region is estimated by a simple and inexpensive method. This is known as sulphation rate measurement technique.

The measurement is made by using lead peroxide and it reacts with sulphur dioxide gives sulphur trioxide. The lead peroxide is pasted over the surface area (100 square centimeter only) of a plastic or glass tube candle. After drying, it is kept at the observation site for a period of 30 days. The sulphation rate is estimated by prescribed gravimetric method. The results are expressed as sulphation rate, as mg of SO_2/100 cm^2/ day. For details, refer Indian Standard for method of measurement of sulphation rate (IS: 5182 (part VIII–1976)).

4.6.4 Estimation of Hydrogen Sulphide from Atmospheric Air

Theory and principles: The hydrogen sulphide in air is estimated by colorimetric method. The principle involved is that the hydrogen sulphide reacts with N, N-dimethyl-p-phenylene diamine, sulphate ferric sulphate and sulphide ions and produce a methylene blue colour. The intensity of colour is proportional to the hydrogen sulphide present in air. The values are reported in the range of 6 to 600 micrograms per cubic meter. Reducing substances like sulphite and thiosulphate prevent the formation of colour. To eliminate them, sufficient amount of ferric sulphate is added. Oxides of nitrogen also interfere, which is eliminated by adding sulphamic acid after sampling.

Sample collection: Using the sampling train equipment, the sample of air (containing hydrogen sulphide) is collected into an impinger which contain 20 ml of absorbing solution at a rate of 1 lpm for 30 min or 0.5 lpm for one hour. After the sampling, cover the impinger with aluminium foil to avoid the exposure to atmosphere.

Preparation of calibration curve: Take 11 tubes of having capacity of 50 ml and filled with 15 ml absorbing solution (annexure III). Add dilute sodium sulphide to each tube, which is sufficient to maintain 1 to 25 micrograms. Also add 1 ml of sulphamic acid, 0.6 ml of N,N-dimethyl-p-phenylene-diamine sulphate solution and 0.05 ml of ferric sulphate solution to each tube and shake them well. Make up the tubes upto 20 ml with distilled water and mix thoroughly. Wait 30 min. for colour development and measure the intensity of colour in a spectrophotometer at 670 nm on transmission scale. Draw the curve based on to transmission values versus micrograms of hydrogen sulphide. Procedure for sample : The same procedure for calibration curve is adopted for sample. The colour of the sample is measured with spectrophotometer and find the micrograms of hydrogen sulphide from calibration chart and its value is expressed as follows.

$$\text{Hydrogen sulphide, } \mu g/m^3 \text{ of air} = \frac{\mu g\, ;\, H_2S \times 1000}{\text{Volume of air, L}}$$

4.6.5 Estimation of Oxides of Nitrogen in Atmospheric Air

Theory and principles: The principle involved in this method is the collection of nitrogendioxide by bubbling the air (which contain nitrogendioxide) through an absorber (sodium hydroxide) solution. It gives a stable sodium nitrite solution. Such nitrite ion produced is made to react with phosphoric acid, sulphanilamide, and N (1-naphtyl) ethylene diamine dihydrochloride, which produce colour. This colour is measured colorimetrically by using spectrophotometer at 540 nm wavelength. The intensity of colour is proportional to the nitrogen dioxide present in the sampled air.

The interference caused by sulphur dioxide is eliminated by treating with hydrogen peroxide which converts sulphurdioxide to sulphuric acid.

Preparation of calibration curve: Prepare solution containing 25 microgram of nitrogen dioxide per ml of absorbent reagent (refer annexure III). Pipette 1, 2, 5, and 15 ml from that solution into 50,

50, 100, and 250 volumetric flasks and dilute to mark with absorbent reagent, which contains 0.5, 1.0, 1.25, and 1.5 micrograms of nitrogendioxide per ml. After gaining colour, measure absorbance at 540 nm wavelength of spectrophotometer and plot absorbance versus micrograms of nitrogen dioxide per ml.

Procedure: By using the sampling train, the sample is collected in a 50 ml of absorber reagent (annexure III) which is kept in an impinger. 10 ml of collected sample is put into a test-tube and add 1 ml of hydrogen peroxide solution and 10 ml of sulphanilamide and 1.4 ml of NEDA solution. In each addition of these reagents, through mixing is done. After 10 minutes colour will be developed and that colour is measured interms of absorbance at 540 nm wavelength of spectrophotometer. The values are read as micrograms of nitrogen dioxide per ml from calibration curve using absorbance values. The results are expressed as follows.

$$NO_2,\ \mu g/m^3 = \frac{(\mu g\ NO_2/ml) \times 50}{V E}$$

where

V = Volume of air sampled, m^3

50 = Volume of absorbent in sampling, ml

E = Fractional overall efficiency, say 0.35

4.6.6 Estimation of Oxidants in Atmospheric Air

Theory and principles: The principle involved in estimation of oxidants (low concentration of ozone plus nitrogendioxide, chlorine, peroxyacetyl nitrate) in air is that the oxidants are made to absorb in potassium iodide solution buffered to a pH of 6.8. Ozone and other organic oxidants liberate iodine, and form trioxide. It produces colour, which is determined by spectrophotometer by measuring absorbance of trioxide ion at 352 nm wave length. Not only ozone but also many oxidizing substances like chlorine, nitrogen dioxide, PAN will liberate iodine. Reducing gases like sulphurdioxide also interfere negatively (increase the value). Nitrogendioxide is estimated to account the interference. The interference of sulphurdioxide is very high, which is eliminated by using a chromic acid paper absorber in the upstream of absorber of sampling train. This method may be used to determine oxidants concentrations in the atmosphere in the range of 0.01 and 10 ppm as ozone.

Collection of sample: The oxidants containing air is sampled by using sampling train and also by placing chromium trioxide paper on the up-stream of absorber. A 10 ml of absorbing solution is placed in an impinger and sampled the air at a rate of 0.5 to 3.0 lpm for 30 min. It gives 2 micrograms of ozone by absorbing solution at an atmospheric concentration of 0.01ppm.

Procedure: Prepare 0.1 to 1.0 ml of 0.0025 N iodine solution in 25 ml volumetric flasks. Dilute to the mark with absorbing solution and mix thoroughly. After 30 min, colour will be developed and its absorbance is measured by using the spectrophotometer at 320 nm wave length. A calibration curve is drawn between absorbance and iodine solution. Similarly % absorbance of the sample is read from the calibration chart. The results are expressed as follows.

$$\text{Oxidants as } (O_3), \text{ ppm.} = AM/V$$

where

A = Corrected absorbance

M = a constant for blank, 0.96

V = Volume of air sample for 10 ml of absorbing solution at 5 °C and 760 mm Hg.

4.6.7 Estimation of Total Fluorides in Atmospheric Air

Theory and principles: Fluorides may be found in air as gas or as particulate matter, which are discharged into the atmosphere through the gaseous effluents of industries like fertilizer, aluminium which use fluoride containing compounds in the manufacturing processess.

The Bureau of Indian Standards recommended two methods for the determination of total fluorides in ambient air.

1. Zirconium SPANDS method
2. Selective Ion Electrode method

1. *Zirconium SPANDS method:* In this method, the fluorides present in air react with metal ion of metal dye complex like Zirconium SPANDS reagent. This reaction will fade the absorbance of the dye solution which is directly proportional to the fluorides present in air. Zirconium SPANDS reagent obey's Beer's law over the range from 0–1.4 micrograms of fluorides per ml, with a detection limit of 0.02 micrograms per ml. Substances like aluminium, iron, phosphate and sulphate ions are causing interference. Hence they have to be eliminated.

Preparation of calibration curve: Prepare a series of fluoride containing solution ranging from 0.1 to 35 micrograms are placed into 25 micro ml volumetric flasks. Add 5 ml of Zirconium-SPANDS reagent to each flask make up to mark and mix the contents thoroughly. Wait for 30 min. for colour gaining and measure the colour interms of absorbances by using spectrophotometer at 570 nm. Draw a curve between fluoride concentration in micrograms and absorbance values.

Procedure: The procedure used for calibration curve may be used for the sample also to get absorbance value.

Results: The concentration of fluorides of the sample are calculated as follows.

$$\text{Fluorides, g/m}^3 = \frac{C \times 1000\ V_t}{V \quad V_a}$$

where

C = Concentration of fluorides in the sample, g

V = Volume of air, L at 25 °C and 760 mm Hg

V_t = Total volume of absorbing solution, ml

V_a = Volume of aliquot taken for sample, ml

For selective Ion Electrode method, please refer IS: 5182 (part xiii)1991.

4.6.8 Estimation of Carbon Monoxide in Atmospheric Air

Theory and principles: In the literature several methods are available for the estimation of carbonmonoxide in air. In the polluted atmosphere, the carbonmonoxide concentration would be around 1 to 100 ppm. No method is reliable to estimate CO for this range of values. Each method is reliable for a certain range of values. Hence, depending on the range of values required, proper method is selected to get accurate values. High values of CO is determined by volumetric gas analysis method, in which CO is oxidised to carbondioxide with hot copper oxide or cuprous salts. Low values are determined by colorimetric methods. But oxidation with iodine pentoxide and colourimetric method by using palladous salts, or ammonium molybdate are widely used methods. However, now a days Non-dispersive infrared Absorption (NDIA) method and gas chromatography methods are preferred for accurate results.

Bureau of Indian Standards recommends four methods. They are as follows.

1. The Indicator tube method is used for routine conditions. CO present in air reduces silicomolybdate (yellow in colour) to lower oxidizing power, which changes yellow to green and green to blue, depending on CO present in air. Interfering substances like hydrogen sulphide, unsaturate hydrocarbons, etc. may present in air, which are eliminated

by providing absorbents in the tubes . This processes is carried by drawing 250 ml of sample of air at a rate of 40 to 50 ml per minute.

2. Iodine pentoxide method
3. Non-dispersive Absorption method, and
4. Gas chromatographic method

For details, refer IS: 5182 (Part X)-1976: Indian Standard for measurement of carbonmonoxide in atmospheric air. The last two methods principles are briefly given below.

NDIA Method: The air sample containing CO is made to pass through the sources of infrared energy and detectors, which are separated by optical cell, where the specific spectral absorption of the component of CO is determined. This arrangements is made in an equipment called 'Infrared Gas Analyser'. This apparatus is suitable for temperature range of 15–40 °C and a relative humidity range of 0 to 99% . The minimum volume of air sample is 2 l and it is collected by sampling train. The results are expressed in units of concentration, which are read from the standard scale.

Gas Chromatography Method: The sample of air containing CO is injected into the gas chromatograph. It is arranged to move one column to other column end. During its movement, the components of air sample are identified by plotting distribution curves and distinct peaks to each gas. Based on peak, the quantity of CO may be estimated. The results are expressed and estimated by comparing peak areas of the sample with peak areas of known amount of constituent of gas chromatograph. The lower detection limit of this method is 10 ppm and the sample size should be 10 ml.

SHORT/FILL UP THE BLANK TYPE QUESTIONS

1. Dust fall jar is used for measuring *particulates* in air.
2. Lead peroxide candle is used for measuring SO_2 in air.
3. *Nephalometry* means the comparison of white light reflected with in a solution containing a suspension.
4. Formazin is used as standard suspension for measuring turbidity.
5. *Turbidity* means the white light transmitted or reflected through a finely divided suspension.
6. Sampling train means an arrangement to *absorb air pollutants* in a *chain* of absorbers *placed in impingers.*
7. The *Durham* sampler collects pollen on a vaseline-coated microscope slide.
8. The *Anderson* sampler collects bacteria and air borne particulates.
9. The Andeson sampler consists of a series of eight stainless steel plates to simulate the human respiratory system that collects particulates which penetrates the alveoli of the lungs.

10. The *Greenberg-Smith* impinger is a glass cylinder with a smaller concentric glass- tube insert. At the bottom of the tube, a glass in jet and a glass impingement structure are immersed in collecting fluid. It is good for capturing particulates greater than 2 microns.
11. The *paper tape* air sampler contains a pump that sucks particulates from the air and deposit on a cellulosic tape filter.
12. *8 to 10* air sampling stations should be located in a city and location of each one is *500 m* away from the stacks.
13. Units of dust fall rate is tons/km^2/month or mg/cm^2 /month.
14. Dust fall rate greater than *20 to 40* tons/km^2/month considered as excessive levels of air pollution.
15. *Isokinetic* velocity is the velocity of gas in the sampling probe and the stack velocity are same while taking the air sampling from a stack.
16. The mean concentration of sulphur dioxide in Bombay is 47 mg/cubic meter. The equivalent concentration in ppm at 25 °C and 1 atmosphere is:
   47 × 24500/(1000000 × 64) = *0.018 ppm.*
17. *Isokinetic sampling* means stack sample taken from a stack at a point where the measured velocity is equal to the effluent velocity in the stack.
18. Concentration of sulphur dioxide is 1 ppm. Its molecular weight is 64. Its concentration is 2620 μg/m^3 at 25 °C and 760 mm Hg.
19. *Lead peroxide* (gravimetric) method is an inexpensive test for measuring average levels of sulphur dioxide.
20. Suspended particulate matter in the air is sampled by high *volume air sampler.*

CHAPTER 5

Meteorology and Air Pollution

5.1 INTRODUCTION

Meteorology is the branch of science which deals with the atmosphere and the characteristic of weather. The planet Earth swings around the Sun in its elliptical orbit and it also rotates on its axis from west to east. The space in between these two (atmosphere) are named as follows.

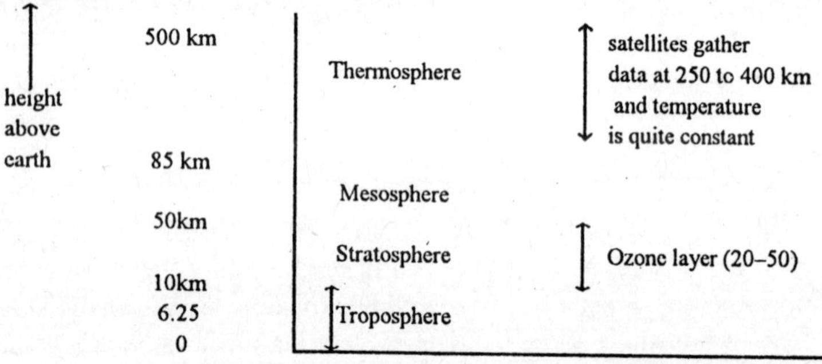

The atmosphere is a fluid mixture of gas surrounding the earth. It consists of several layers of varying thickness and density. The layer nearest to the earth is called troposphere, which extends 6.25 km from the earth's surface. The lower troposphere (upto 2 km), which is the most relevant to air pollution. The solar energy reaches the earth through space as electromagnetic waves. Most of this radiation is absorbed by the water vapour in the atmosphere. A part of the heat energy that reaches the earth surface is reradiated back into the atmosphere which is absorbed by the carbondioxide and water vapour.

The spherical shape of the earth allows the sun's rays to strike with more intensity at the equator and less at the poles. So heat of air is more at the equator and less at the poles. The differential heating of air creates horizontal pressure gradient, results horizontal motion of air in the atmosphere. The deflecting forces acting on a body in motion due to earth's rotation are called as coriolis forces. Large scale motions of the air occurs due to temperature differences between the atmosphere at poles and at the equator. Warm air moves towards east from tropics to poles and cold air moves toward west from poles to equator. In the northern hemisphere the counter clockwise motion of air around a low pressure centre which is termed as cyclones. The clockwise motion around a high pressure centre is termed as anticyclone. If the earth surface is considered as curved one, and even in the curved path, the speed of the air may be constant. Based on this, gradient wind is the wind resulting from the resultant force of pressure forces and coriolis forces. The movement of air near the earth's surface is affected by the frictional forces. The wind speed must be zero at the earth's surface (flow velocity must be zero on the surface of an air foil) and the gradient wind occurs at a few hundred meters above the ground level.

5.2 WIND VELOCITY

The change in velocity with altitude depends on the type of terrain and time of that location. The nature of the terrain, the location and density of trees, the location and size of water bodies and buildings produce different wind velocity gradients along the latitiudes. The wind velocity profiles are shown in Fig. 5.1

From the figures it can be seen that the air flow is smooth and sharp when the surface is smooth. Rough surfaces can generate more mechanical turbulence which creates eddies and the eddy motion effect the dispersion of pollutants in air. The type of eddy formations are shown in Fig.5.2

Thermal turbulence give rises to very large eddies, which results large motions of plume, but little dispersion occurs. Small eddeys will increase the plume size slowly. In the Atmosphere different eddy sizes are present which disperse the plume in a meander fashion along the wind direction.

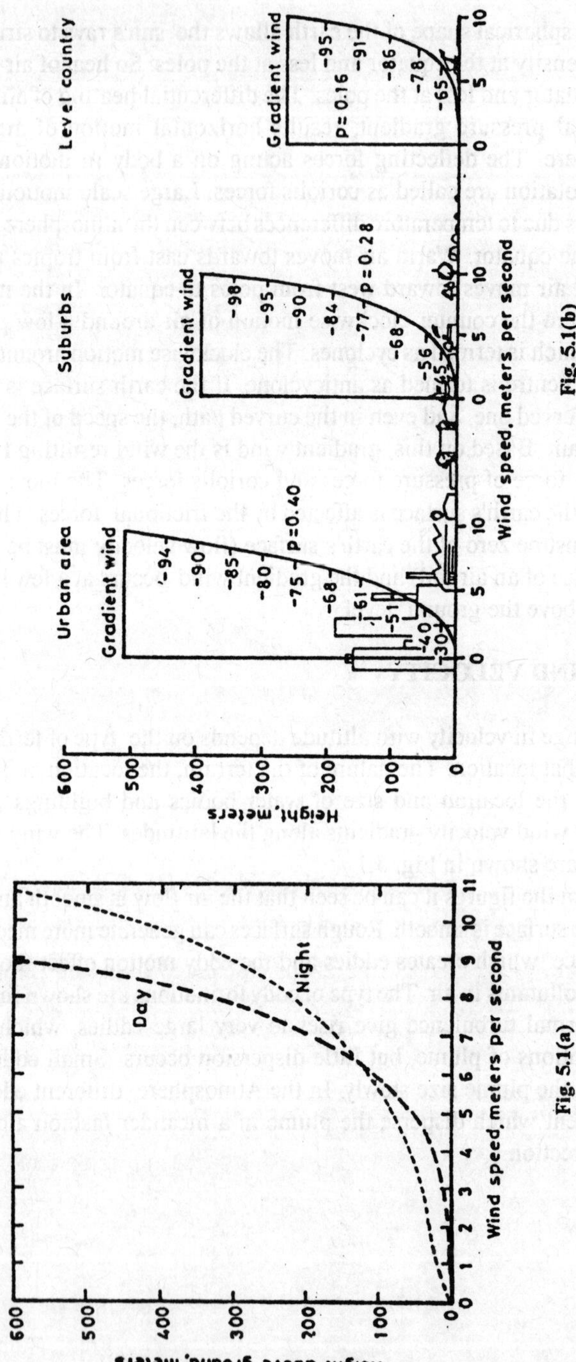

Fig. 5.1(a)

Fig. 5.1(b)

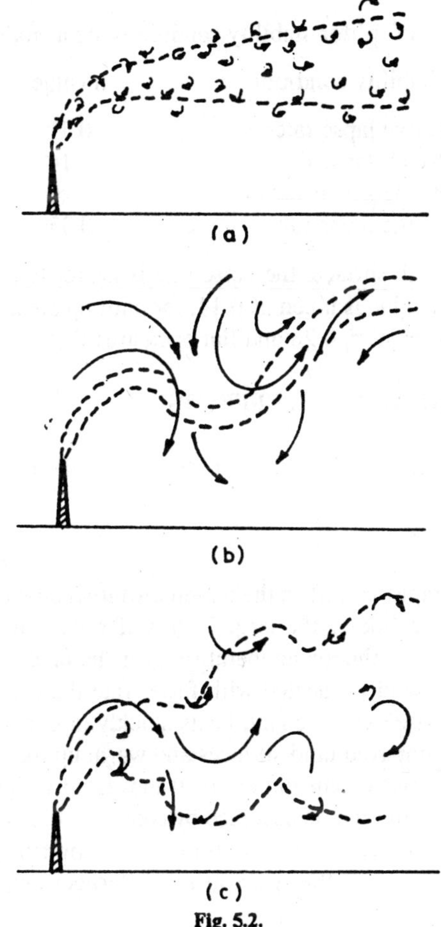

Fig. 5.2.

So the wind direction at a height is calculated based on 'power law' which as follows.

$$(U/U_1) = (Z/Z_1)_n$$

Where

U = wind speed at altitude, Z

U_1 = wind speed at altitude, Z_1

n = a constant, which varies 0.12 to 0.5 depending on atmospheric conditions

The values of 'n' for stability conditions are as follows

Stability condition	n value
Large lapse rates	0.11
Small lapse rates	0.14
Moderate inversion	0.20
Large inversion	0.33

For a smooth surface, the lapse rate is nearer to A.L.R.(Adiabatic Lapse Rate), n value is taken as 0.14, for built up areas n = 0.4, suburbs n = 0.28 and flat open area n = 0.16.

5.3 TOPOGRAPHICAL EFFECTS

Oceans, mountains, valleys, and buildings will influence the air motion.

1. Ocean Winds

Surface topography can effect the sea-breeze either on-shore or off-shore. Along the shore line of the large bodies of water (like sea, lake etc.) during sunney day the air temperature over the land is more than the ocean because land is heated with faster rate than water. On the day time (hot sun-rise day), the land heats quickly (absorbs solar radiation fastly) over a unpaved land surfaces and warm up the air over the land surface to give rise expansion of air. It moves up which creates a low-pressure region and that is occupied by cooler air blowing from the sea. The on-shore sea breeze (breeze from the sea towards shore) develops during the day and reaches peak at mid afternoon, which is shown in Fig.5.3.

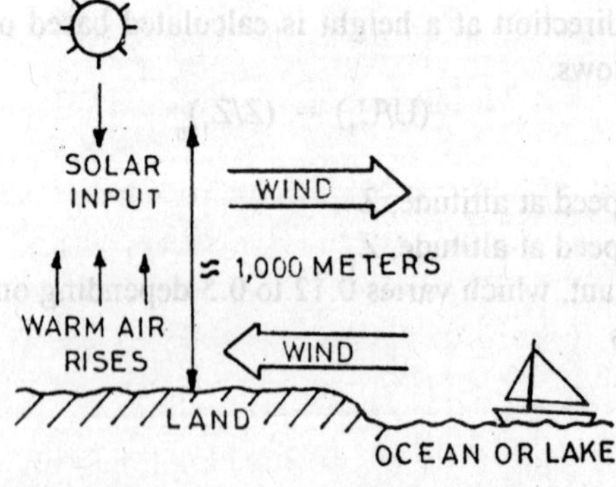

Fig. 5.3.

After sunset, the temperature of air over the land (shore) decreases with a faster rate because the rate of cooling of earth surface is more than water. At night the ocean is relatively warmer than the land (shore), hence the off-shore breeze develops during night and moves from land to warm sea.

If power plants are located on the sea-coast, the stack effluents will be dispersed over the land during day time by on-shore sea breeze and may be subjected to fumigation (dispersion of pollutnats towards ground level).

2. Mountain-Valley Winds

During day time, air over the base and mountain slopes is heated up by solar radiation and begins to rise and flows over the valley and mountain slopes. After sunset the earth's surfaces looses solar radiation heat quickly. The cooling of earth suface and air surrounding it give rises to change in density of air. As the night proceeds the air along the valley slopes become dense, colder and moves downward into the valley as a slopes wind. This cold, dense air occupy the valley and tendency to move along the valley axis.

If heavy air pollutant emitting industries are located in the valley, the pollutants are trapped in the valley. During the night the cold air occupied in the valley and warm air occupies at high altitude of the valley. So stable conditions prevail which leads to formation of inversions (trapping of pollutants at a height and they can not move by stable conditions). During the day time also the plume (pollutant dispersion) would move up to the valley only. They return to the valley at the nights since the wind shifts towards the lower end of the valley. This circulation of wind may give rise to the build up of the pollutants concentration to dangerous levels.

3. Obstacles Like Buildings

The characteristics of the land surrounding a stack and the location, non-uniform heights of buildings relative to stack height will influence upon the behaviour of a plume and the generation of mechanical turbulence. Different types of conditions are presented below.

(i) Location of Stack behind the Hill or Building

- Location of stack or chimney behind a hill may allow the effluents to down wash which is shown in Fig.5.4. But the plume may rise above

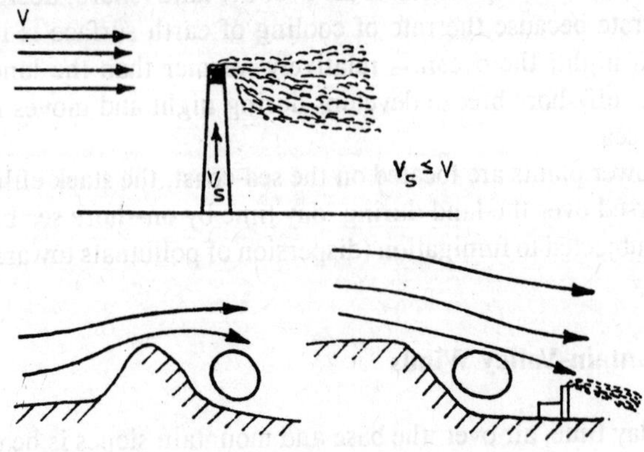

Fig. 5.4.

the stack level. If the stack gas velocity is equal to or less than the ambient velocity, the pollutants may be carried downward on the backside of the stack. Similarly the wind flow pattern around a building is shown in Fig. 5.5.

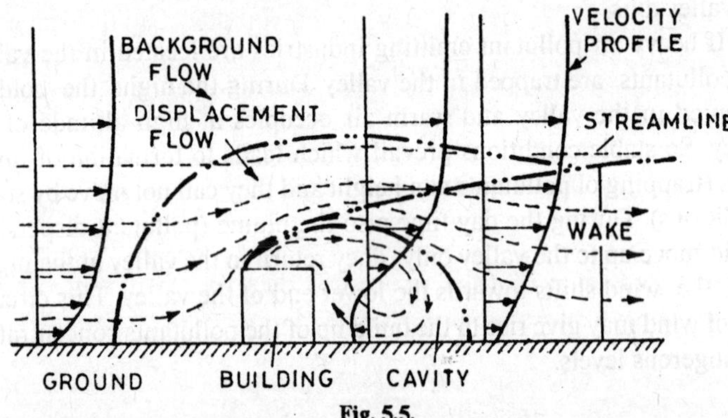

Fig. 5.5.

Due to sudden obstruction (structure), the flow separates to form a cavity behind the building. The backwash of flow is behind the structure. Back flow can occur within the cavity. If pollutant entered in this region tends to remain. If flow reverses in its direction near the ground level, separation can occur on the backside of the building.

(ii) Location of Stack Before the Structure (Hill or Building)

When a stack is placed upwind of the hill or building (stack before the structure) wake behind a structure will influence the plume behaviour, as seen in Fig. 5.6(a) and (b).

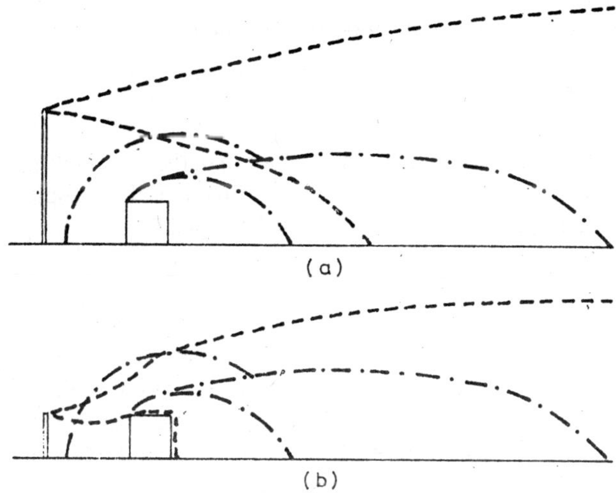

Fig. 5.6(a) and (b).

If the stack height is more as shown in Fig. 5.6(a), the plume may be away from the cavity behind the structure (building). The wake behind the building will help to increase the turbulence so that more dispersion will take place.

If the stack height is not sufficient shown in Fig. 5.6(b) the plume enters the cavity. High pollutant concentrations accumulate along the backside of the building. Hence the designer has to visualise the influence of topography in fixing the stack height. As a thumb rule, stack height, H near the building should be greater than or equal to 2.5 times the height of the building.

5.4 ATMOSPHERIC STABILITY

Earth's surface absorbs solar radiation and a part of it reradiate to the atmosphere. So the air is warmed near the earth's surface, the molecules of air become agitated and push away from one another. This causes the air for expansion and become less dense and exerts less pressure than the cold air.

The air near the earth surface is heated up and expands. This expansion pressurise the nearby cold air to give way to warm air to move up. These temperature differences create inequality in pressure which causes the air to flow from the region of high pressure (near the earth) to the règions of low pressure (at high altitudes). At equator, temperature is high and less at poles. The temperature in between them varies, giving warmer in the summer and colder in the winter.

Unstable

If the rising parcel of air remains warmer than the surrounding air, the parcel of air will continue to rise in the direction of its displacement. Such an atmosphere condition is said to be unstable.

Stable

If the rising parcel of air is colder, denser than the surrounding air, air parcel pushes downward and over against the direction of displacement. Such an atmosphere condition is said to be stable. The stability is a function of vertical distribution of atmosphere temperature.

Pressure Systems

The air has weight, so the whole atmosphere pushes down upon the earth's surface. This pressure is measured with an instrument called mecury barometer . It measures the weight for a unit area of a column of air extending to the top of the atmosphere.

At, 45 °N, 0 °C, 760 mm of Hg is defined as 1 atmosphere. The air pressure rises or fall depending on the location, roughness of the surface,, radiation, and wind.

High Pressure Systems

These are related to the clear skies, light winds and stable atmosphere. In the northern hemisphere, the vertical motion of air is downward and horizontal motion is clockwise.

Low Pressure System

These are related to cloudy skies, gusty wind, atmospheric instability and the formation of fronts. In the northern hemisphere horizontal air movement is counter clockwise and vertical movement is upward.

5.5 LAPSE RATES

The decrease of temperature with altitude is called as 'lapse rate', (-dt/dz). The lapse rate in the atmosphere is called as actual lapse rate or prevailing lapse rate or atmospheric lapse rate or environmental lapse rate or simply 'lapse rate' or ambient lapse rate.

Dry Adiabatic Lapse Rate (DALR)

Consider a parcel of hot air releases into the atmosphere. The air tends to expand and rise untill it reaches a level where the hot air temperature and density is equal to that of surrounding air. In general, the process of expansion is usually very rapid. So, it can be assumed that it occurs with no heat transfer between the parcel of hot air and the surrounding atmosphere. The change in temperature with altitude is due to adiabatic (without any heat transfer) cooling. Hence, the decrease of temperature with altitude without loss or gain of heat from the surroundings is called DRY ADIABATIC LAPSE RATE. The rate of temperature change from the origin of hot air to the point of attaining equal temperature is called ambient lapse rate.

The adiabatic lapse rate of an ideal gas is approximately 1°C per 100 m (5.4°F per 1000 feet), which is used for comparing the environmental lapse rates in a particular location. The dry adiabatic lapse rate as per the international convention of U.S.A. is approximately 0.66°C per 100 m (3.6°F per 1000 feet).

The different types of lapse rates are shown in Fig. 5.7(a) to (d).

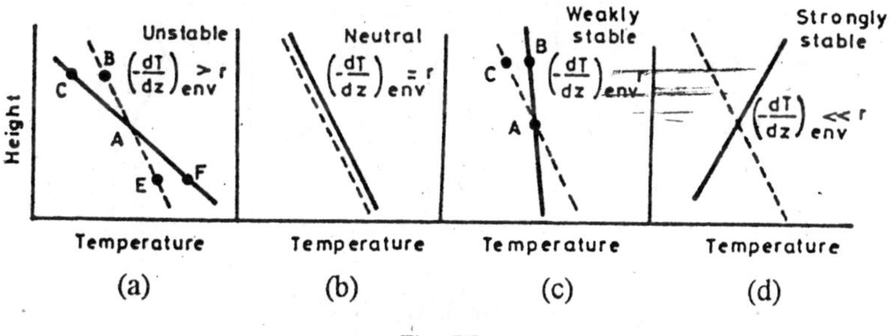

Fig. 5.7.

If the environmental lapse rate is more than the DALR, it is called as super adiabatic lapse rate. If the environmental lapse rate is less than DALR, it is called as sub adiabatic lapse rate. If the environmental lapse rate is exactly DALR, it is called as neutral lapse rate. When the lapse rate is zero for a layer of air, is called as isothermal, which means that there is no change in temperature with height. If the temperature of the air at earth's surface is cooler than thetemperature at high altitudes in an area, then the temperature increases with altitude which is called as negative lapse rate or INVERSION.

An atmosphere is said to be stable when the environmental lapse rate is less than the dry adiabatic lapse rate. In a stable atmospherc, pollutants are slowly dispersed and vertical motion is very less. Atmospheric condition with super adiabatic lapse rate is said to be unstable. In that condition, the density of air is less than the surroundings, so the air continue to rise up.

5.6 INVERSIONS

Two types of inversions are most commonly exist. They are as follows.
(i) Subsidence inversion, and
(ii) Radiation inversion or temperature inversion

(i) Subsidence Inversion

This type if inversion which is shown in Fig. 5.8(a) is formed by the subsidence or sinking of the air in high pressure area (anitcyclones) at moderate altitudes. The sinking of air to lower altitudes compresses the

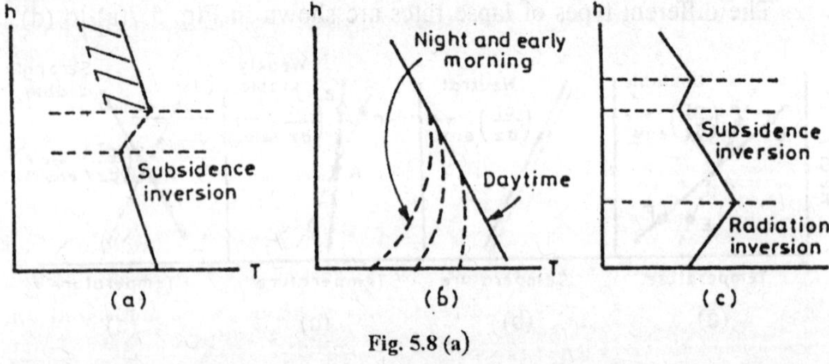

Fig. 5.8 (a)

nearby layer and increases the temperature. The top layer is warming more rapidly than the bottom of the layer. If the subsidence of the layer continue for sufficient time, a positive temperature gradient negative lapse rate) will be created within the layer, which creates an inversion. This is called subsidence inversion.

(ii) Radiation Inversion

This is shown in Fig. 5.8(b). In a cloud free atmosphere, during day time, air near the earth's surface receives more heat by radiation and become more warmer during late morning and afternoon. After sunset, the earth's surface looses the heat and quickly cools as the night starts. The air layers adjacent to the earth's surface are cooled to a temperature less than that of high altitudes. After mid night and early morning, the negative lapse rate is formed (increase of temperature with altitude). The formation of inversion is due to temperature or radiation hence, it is called as radiation inversion or temperature inversion. This will breaks up as the morning sun heats the ground and warm air moves up. Subsidence and radiation inversions may occur at a time as shown in Fig. 5.8(c).

5.7 PLUME BEHAVIOUR

Under different atmospheric conditions, the plume behaviour is classified into six types which are shown in Fig. 5.9.

In the atmosphere when the lapse rate is super adiabatic, a looping plume Fig. 5.9(a)occurs. It is usually associated with a clear day time with strong solar heating of the earth's surface with light winds.

A coning plume Fig. 5.9(b) occurs when the atmosphere condition is with a lapse rate less than super adiabatic and with moderate to strong winds and the skies are with cloud cover during day and night.

In a stable atmosphere negative lapse rates prevails, which gives an inversion to a considerable distance. So a fanning plume which is shown n Fig. 5.9(c).

If an inversion layer lies below over an unstable layer, a lofting plume occurs as shown in Fig. 5.9(d). In this conditions the pollutants are dispersed without any ground level concentrations. Inversions are the characteristic of clear night time conditions when the earth is cooled by outgoing radiations. It is a condition, predecessor to fumigation.

A fumigation plume occurs as shown in Fig. 5.9(e) when a stable layer of air present over a short distance just above the stack and an unstable air layer below it. It usually exists in the early morning following a night with a stable inversion.

When an inversion exists both below and above the stack height, a trapping plume results which is shown in Fig. 5.9(f).

STACK HEIGHT AND MIXING DEPTH

Dispersion of effluents from a stack or a chimney is primarily a function of the stability of the atmosphere and stack height. The ground level concentrations of pollutants at a point on the downstream side from the

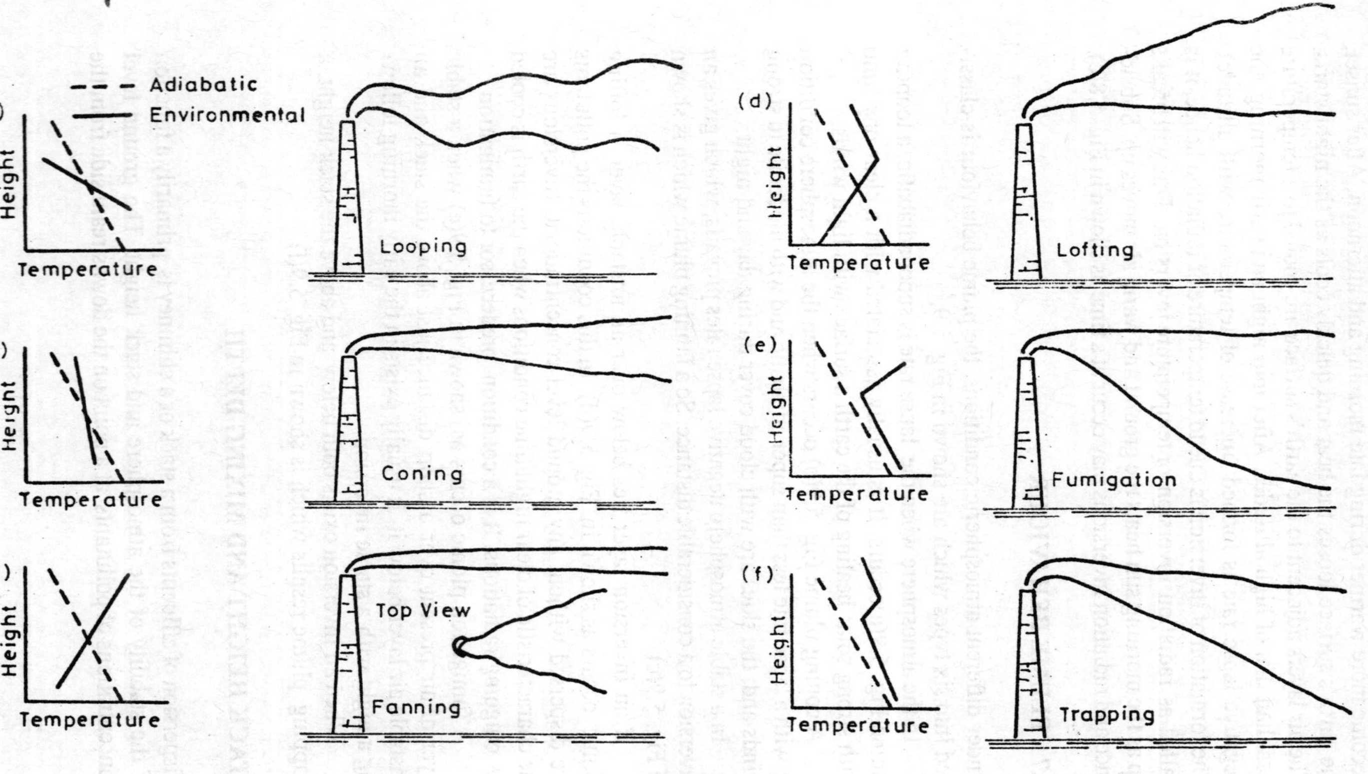

Adiabatic
Environmental
a)
Height
Temperature
Looping
(b)
Height
Temperature
Coning
(c)
Height
Temperature
Top View
Fanning
(d)
Height
Temperature
Lofting
(e)
Height
Temperature
Fumigation
(f)
Height
Temperature
Trapping

Fig. 5.9.

stack is a function of stack height. More height of the stack, lesser the ground level concentrations. In calculating the GLCs, the effecting stack height has considered. This is defined as follows.

Effective stack height, He = H + ΔH (5.2)

where,

H= physical stack height,

ΔH = plume rise

Mixing depth: Height available for the mixing of pollutants are known as mixing depth.

Maximum Mixing Depth (MMD): Maximum mixing depths are calculated based on the data for a month. An average period of months is calculated called as mean maximum mixing depth (MMMD). The altitude at which the dry adiabatic line intersects is taken as MMD. The value of MMD are lowest at night and increase at day. Under a severe inversion at night, the MMD value may be zero.

5.8. MACRO AND MICRO METEOROLOGY

Depending on the magnitude, wind circulation in an area, meteorology may be divided into tow types.

1. Macrometeorology (large scale movement of air)
2. Micrometeorology (small scale movement of air)

Macrometeorology means the movement of large masses of air. This occurs due to variation in temperature, pressure and rotation of earth. At equator, the air is warmer and cooler at poles. This temperature variation tends to disperse while the earth is rotated. Atmospheric pressure, temperature, humidity, wind speed and direction, clouds etc. will influence the global movement of air masses.

Micrometeorology means the studying of air circulation and temperature in a region like valleys, slopes of mountains, buildings and trees and ground cover. These will influence the dispersion of pollutants. Information about the wind speed and direction of a location is essential to predict the dispersion of pollutants usually this is represented by wind roses.

Wind roses: Wind roses is a graphical representation of wind data giving the % frequencies of wind speed, wind direction for a given location. Wind roses are prepared for each month. A typical wind rose is shown in Fig. 5.10.

The typical data is given in Table 5.1 and the procedure is as follows.

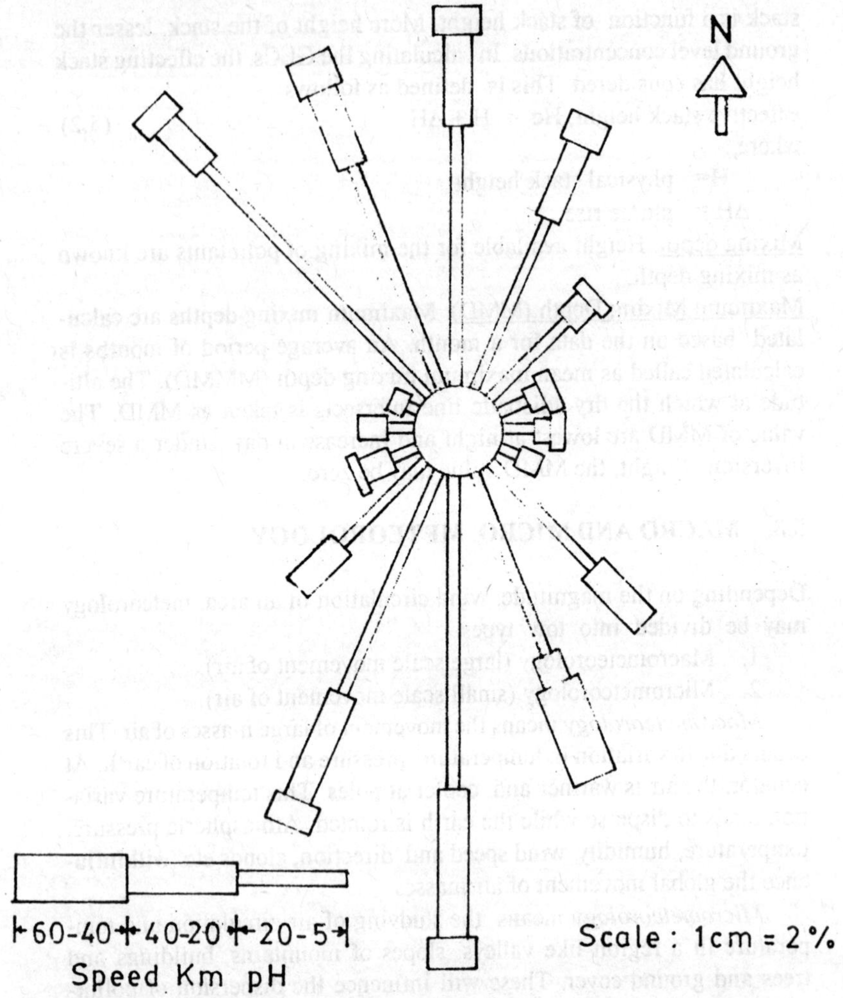

Fig. 5.10.

Wind rose diagram: Wind blows at a particular location (say station) with varying speeds and directions with time. It is very essential to present its position with time for air pollution studies, which is generally represented on paper by diagram. Wind rose diagram is a graphical representation of wind data giving the % frequencies of wind speed, wind direction for a given location. They may be drawn for a day, a month, and for a year. The data required for drawing the wind rose diagram is wind speed, period of blowing and wind direction. The wind data is usually recorded and maintained by the meteorological departments of the government. Data are usually reported at eight primary and eight secondary directions of the compass. The wind speed is also divided into certain ranges. The % of wind blowing in a particular direction is calculated as follows.

$$\% \text{ of frequency of wind} = \frac{\text{period of wind blowing, h}}{\text{unit period, say 24 hrs.}} \times 100$$

These are entered on a sheet as shown in example.

Example: Table 5.1

Draw a wind rose diagram for the following data:

Wind Data								
Wind direction	Duration of wind speed, h				% duration of wind speed			
	5-20 KMPH	20-40 KMPH	40-60 KMPH	Total	5-20 KMPH	20-40 KMPH	40-60 KMPH	Total
Column 1	2	3	4	5	6	7	8	9
N	1.56	0.72	0.12	2.4	6.5	3.0	0.5	10.0
N-NE	1.20	0.55	0.17	1.92	5.0	2.3	0.7	8.0
NE	0.72	0.114	0.072	0.936	3.0	0.6	0.3	3.9
E-NE	0.24	0.096	0.048	0.384	1.0	0.4	0.2	1.6
E	0.19	0.074	0.048	0.312	0.8	0.3	0.2	1.3
E-SE	1.2	0.072	–	0.192	0.5	0.3	–	0.8
SE	0.96	0.48	–	1.44	4.0	2.0	–	6.0
S-SE	1.20	0.84	–	2.04	5.0	3.5	–	8.5
S	2.02	0.96	0.14	3.12	8.4	4.0	0.6	13.0
S-SW	1.63	0.72	0.05	2.40	6.8	3.0	0.2	10.0
SW	0.72	0.36	–	1.08	3.0	1.5	–	4.5
W-SW	0.24	0.19	0.05	0.48	1.0	0.8	0.2	2.0
W	0.19	0.17	–	0.36	0.8	0.7	–	1.5
W-NW	0.144	0.048	–	0.192	0.6	0.2	–	0.8
NW	2.16	0.288	0.192	2.64	9.0	1.2	0.8	11.0
N-NW	1.68	0.552	0.192	2.424	7.0	2.3	0.8	10.1
								93.0

Solution: Column 1 to 5 from data recorded:

Column 6:

$$\text{Ist reading: \% duration of wind blowing} = \frac{\text{period (col. 2), h}}{24} \times 100$$

$$= \frac{1.56}{24} \times 100 = 6.5$$

column 7 and 8: same procedure as column 6, using column 3 and 4 respectively.
column 9: total of columns 6, 7, and 8
Ist reading (i.e.) = 6.5 + 3.0 + 0.5 = 10.0
Add all values of column 9. Generally it will be less than 100, in this example it is 93
The difference of 100 and 93 (i.e.), = 7% accounts for the wind speed less than 5 KMPH. This is considered as calm and shown it as encircle (not to scale) in the diagram as shown in Fig. 5.10.
Select a suitable scale say 1 cm = 2% duration of wind speed and suitable width (not to scale) for differentiate different wind speed. For example,
In the northern direction

Speed, KMPH	% wind speed	scale	length of arm, cm
5–20	6.5	1cm = 2%	3.25
20–40	3.0		1.50
40–60	0.5		0.25
	10.0	total arm length	5.0

Similarly, the length of distribution arms of diagram is calculated for all the directions and complete wind rose diagram is drawn. For the data given in this example, the diagram is shown in Fig.5.10.

5.9 METEOROLOGICAL INSTRUMENTS

The pressure, temperature, humidity, wind speed and direction in a specified time and location have to be measured for studying the effects of air pollution.
Atmospheric pressure: The atmospheric pressure is measured by mercury barometer and the values are expressed as height of mercury in mm (mm of Hg).
Temperature: It is measured by thermometer, expressed as Celcius degrees or in Kelvins.
Humidity: The humidity of atmosphere is measured by psychrometer. This consists of tow thermometers. The bulb of one thermometer is covered with a wet cloth and whirled in the air. The other one is dry condition. From the temperature difference between the dry bulb and wet bulb thermometers, the humidity is calculated.
Wind speed and direction: The wind speed is measured by cup

anemometers. The rate of rotation of the shaft to which cups are attached is indicated on a scale. The unit of expression is Kmph.

Surface wind direction is measured by a wind vane. It is a flat plate on a horizontal rods, which aligns itself with direction. The wind direction aloft (at very height) is determined by pilot balloons (pibals) which are generally less than 1m diameter, equipped to carry a small radio for tracking.

The standard elevation for wind instruments is 10 m above ground level in an open terrain (Available clear distance is 10 times the height of the obstacle).

Solar Radiation: Pyrheliometer is used to measure solar radiation. This instrument measures the temperature difference (by thermocouples) between two concentric rings own with a blacked surface and other with a whitened surface.

SHORT/FILL UP THE BLANK TYPE QUESTIONS

1. Decrease of temperature of air with increasing of altitude is called *lapse rate.*
2. In dry air, the adiabatic lapse rate is *0.98 °C per 100 m.*
3. Solar heating causes turbulence in air is called *thermal* turbulence.
4. A negative lapse rate or increase in air temperature with increase in altitude is called *inversion.*
5. Commonly inversions are two types, namely *radiation* inversion and *subsidence* inversion.
6. A *radiation* inversion usually occurs at night when the earth's surface is cooled by radiation at a faster rate than the air.
7. *Subsidence* inversions are normally caused by the sinking motion in high pressure areas.
8. High pressure area air descends, it compresses and increases in temperature. This may result in the upper air becoming warmer than the lower air thus producing *inversion* near the land surfaces.
9. Air motion caused over rough surface of the earth is called *mechanical* turbulence.
10. Water vapour is normally present in air in the range of *1 to 3%* by volume.
11. Wind speed below 1.5 kilometer per hour is considered as *calm.*
12. *Fumigation* type of plumes create worst pollution situations at ground level.
13. The *micro meteorology* deals with the study of minute changes in atmosphere conditions confined to a limited area of few square km and upto 1000 m height.
14. *Dry adiabatic lapse rate* is the rate of cooling with lifting/decent of a parcel of air without any heat exchange with the surroundings.
15. In summer, the land near the coast warms up during the day time and heats the air layer above it. As the warm air rises, draws the cool air from the sea causes *inversion* near the coast.
16. During night radiation inversions occur over the land near the coast due to the *land* and *sea breeze effects.*
17. *Radiation inversion* means inversions result through a loss of heat from earth by radiation at a faster rate than by normal cooling of air.

18. Radiation inversions usually occurs *at nights.*
19. *Inversion* is an atmospheric condition in which a layer of cool air is trapped by a layer of warm air.
20. *Wind rose* is a graphic display of the distribution of wind speed and direction experienced at a given location.
21. Hourly wind speeds and directions for a specific period of a month or an year are plotted as a *wind rose* for the region.
22. *Wind roses* are used to choose sites for the location of industries based on the winds.
23. High pressure systems are related to *clear skies, light* winds and *stable* atmosphere.
24. Low pressure system are associated with *unstable* atmosphere conditions and commonly brings winds and rain.
25. Detecting forces acting on a body in motion due to earth's rotation is called *coriolis force.*
26. If there is no rotation of earth, air normally would tend to flow directly from *high pressure* region towards *low pressure* region, which is horizontally from a *cold* area toward a warm area.
27. Isobars means *lines of constant pressure.*
28. Wind resulting from the resultant force of pressure forces and coriolis forces is called as *gradient wind.*
29. As the hot air expands, it become less dense and exerts less pressure than cold air. As the hot air expands, the cooler air next to it will be under greater pressure pushes sideways forcing the warmer air upward. This temperature difference creates *pressure difference* causing air to flow from *high pressure* regions to *low pressure* regions.
30. The land heats quickly, expanding the air and creating a *low pressure* area and that is filled by cooler air blowing *from the sea.* When the sun sets, land cools and the wind blows *sea ward* in coastal areas.
31. To prevent the induced flow of stack pollutants toward the ground in the vicinity of a building, the stack height should be at least *2.5 times the height of the building.*
32. Effluents form chimneys or stack may also become trapped in the wake, it is then known as *down wash.*
33. The air layer that is influenced by friction extends from a few hundred meters to several kilometers above the surface of the earth is called *planetary boundary layer.*
34. Measure of ability of the atmosphere to disperse the emitted pollutants is expressed as *degree of stability.*
35. In the northern hemisphere, the air blow *counter clockwise* around low pressure centres.
36. The earth emits heat in the form of *long* wave radiation.
37. When the lapse rate is Zero for a layer of air, it is termed as *isothermal.*
38. An atmosphere with nearer to an adiabatic lapse rate is called as *neutral stability.*
39. At neutral stability, displaced mass of air neither tends to return its *original* position nor tends to continue its *displaced* position.
40. A volume of air reaches its new position at exactly the temperature of the surroundings, then the prevailing lapse rate is said to be exactly the same as *adiabatic lapse rate.*
41. When the temperature increases with altitude, the lapse rate is negative and the atmospheric condition is termed as *inversion.*
42. Radiation inversions are most likely to occur during *cloudless* and *windless* nights.
43. Radiation inversions are suppressed by an appreciable *cloud* cover and by *strong* winds.
44. Radiation inversion frequently occur upto height is less than *500* meters.
45. Subsidence and radiation inversion leads to a phenomenon called *trapping* of a stack plume.

46. The warming of the air in the morning over a land mass will induce the flow of cooler air toward the land from an adjacent *large lake or ocean.* This results in *warmer* air aloft and a *cooler* layer air along the surface of an *inversion* condition.
47. The warm front frequently will tend to override the more dense, cooler air ahead of it, thus creating a localised *temperature* inversion.
48. A passage of cold front into and under a warm region ahead of it will lead a *temperature* inversion.
49. A clear hot day accompanied by light winds may produce a *looping* plume.
50. With moderate to strong winds and turbulence largely mechanical rather than thermal a *conning* piume may be expected.
51. In a very stable atmosphere, the stack effluents form a *fanning* plume.
52. In the morning, warming up of ground surface, stable atmosphere becomes which reaches a fanning plume light to moderate winds forces the heavy concentrated pollutants to the ground, which forms a *fumigation* plume.
53. Maximum mixing depth is approximately is *500* m.
54. When an inversion occurs aloft, a *trapping* plume may be found.
55. *The mixing height* is a measure of the vertical distance available for the mixing of pollutants and it accounts for the effect of inversions.
56. MMD means Maximum Mixing Depth which is defined as *the average of the highest mixing heights available.*
57. *Looping* plume occurs when the lapse rate is super adiabatic and the air is turbulent.
58. *Looping* plume occurs during warm seasons with clear skies when solar insolation is high.
59. *Coning* occurs when large rate is sub-adiabatic but less than isothermal.
60. *Coning* is likely to occur with overcast or night skies and moderate Wind speeds.
61. *Fanning* occurs when the temperature gradient is positive.
62. *Fanning* is after the predecessor to fumigation condition.
63. *Lofting* occurs when an inversion exists only below the plume and the plume is inhibited from mixing downward.
64. *Trapping* occurs when the plume is caught between inversions.
65. Inversion grows upto stack height, lofting conditions change to *fanning.*
66. Stack in warm, dry climates will exhibit *looping* in the after noon.
67. Stack in warm, dry climates, depending on stack height *lofting or fanning* plume occurs in the early morning hours.
68. Cloudy, wet conditions give rises to *coning* plume.
69. The heat energy in the atmosphere comes from the Sun as *short wave* radiation.
70. Leaves rustle means the wind velocity is considered as *light (5 to 10 kmph).*
71. Moderate (dust risen) winds means *20 to 30 kmph* and strong (whole tree moves) winds means *50 to 60 kmph.*
72. Effective stack height = physical height of stack plus *plume rise.*
73. Fanning plume is formed during *inversions.*
74. Ideally a parcel of air cools at about 2.83 °K/km as it ascending.
75. When the surface of air is *warmer* than a layer of air below it, mixing does not take place.
76. The wind speed which is almost ineligible at the earth's surface increases to a considerable value with height and is called as *gradient wind.*
77. When the inversion exists below the point of emission of pollutant with a normal lapse rate above that point of emission a *lofting* plume occurs.
78. *Subsidence* inversion results in because of slow moving high pressure areas.
79. When the adiabatic lapse rate occurs upto the top of the chimney stack and inverted lapse rate above it then *fumigation* plume results.

80. Tall stacks, high wind velocities and *turbulent unstable* air is conducive for rapid dilution of the pollutants.
81. In a *lofting* plume, the inversion acts as a lid and protects the ground surface from fumigation.
82. When the atmosphere is *highly unstable*, the greatest amount of spreading of smoke takes place.
83. An inversion is said to be formed when the ambient temperature *increases* with altitude.
84. When the parcel of air accelerates its upward motion the atmosphere is said to be *unstable* and mixing between the layers is encouraged.
85. A *fumigation* plume is a feature of chimneys discharging effluents into an unstable air flow and can results in bad air pollution at ground level.
86. Wind is a result of an equilibrium produced by pressure, *coriolis* and friction forces.
87. Air pollution control is concerned with the lower portion of *troposphere.*
88. Sea breeze developes during *mid-afternoon.*
89. Coriolis force is a force due to the rotation of the earth.
90. With reference to air pollution studies, pibal (pilot balloons) is released for measuring *lapse rate and direction of wind at stack height.*
91. Average wind direction at stack height is measured by *pibal by tracking the balloon by one or more theodolites on the ground.* Average wind direction is obtained by triangulation method.
92. Upslope and downslope winds and sea-breeze are caused by local geographical and *topography* features and occur over a *mountain - valley and oceans.*
93. Heat island effect: In a city, the warm air tends to be concentrated at the centre of the city, rises upward and carries the air pollutants. After reaching certain height, it expands and flows towards the outskirts of the city due to cool air in the surrounding area and finally cools. That cool air at the outskirts will return back towards the centre of the city, due to temperature difference where it warms up and expands and rises up. This cycle is repeated and heat island is formed, in that area. It will be continued untill a strong wind breaks the cycle. This is shown in Fig. 5.11.

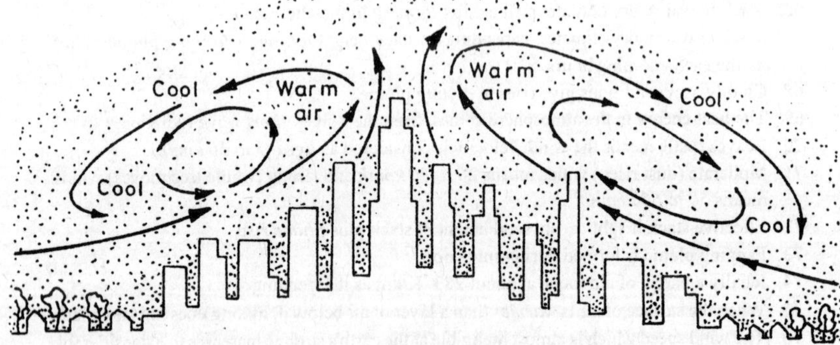

Fig. 5.11.

94. Sun rays are scattered by air molecules and they have different wavelengths that gives a clear sky with *deep blue colour.*
95. Sun rays are scattered more near the horizon which produces *reddish* sunrises and sun-sets.
96. Troposphere is heated primarily from the *ground* but not from the *sun.*
97. Sun rays are absorbed by ozone, water vapour, carbondioxide dust and clouds of lower *tropo* sphere.

CHAPTER 6

Modelling of Dispersion of Pollutants

6.1 INTRODUCTION

Pollutants either gases or particulate matter with gases are released into the atmosphere through stacks. If the size of particulate matter is less than or equal to twenty microns, they move approximately same as gas dispersion. The dispersion (spreading phenomena) of pollutants in the atmosphere is depended upon so many interrelated parameters like (a) nature of the pollutants (b) meteorological conditions of the area and (c) nature of the terrain on the downstream side of the stack, etc. It is essential to predict the dispersion of pollutants which enables to assess the ambient air quality of an area. Mathematical models have been developed to predict the ground level concentrations or dispersion of the pollutants based on assumptions.

6.2 DISPERSION MODELS

In the literature of air pollution, it is found that several mathematical equations of dispersion are available. They describe about the transport and dispersion of air pollutants in the atmosphere. These formulae have been developed based on certain assumptions. One such popular equation is 'Gaussian dispersion model'.

6.2.1 Gaussian Dispersion Model

The Gaussian dispersion model is an equation developed for a partial differential equation of mass transport and dispersion of an elemental volume in the direction of wind. While deriving the model, the following assumptions are made:

(i) The concentration of the pollutants releases from a continuous point source and with a steady state.

(ii) Wind speed is constant at any point in x, y, and z co-ordinate system and

(iii) The major distribution of pollutant due to wind lies along the x-axis.

Gaussian dispersion model is based on the norma! or Gaussian probability distribution function and its co-ordinate system is shown in Fig. 6.1.

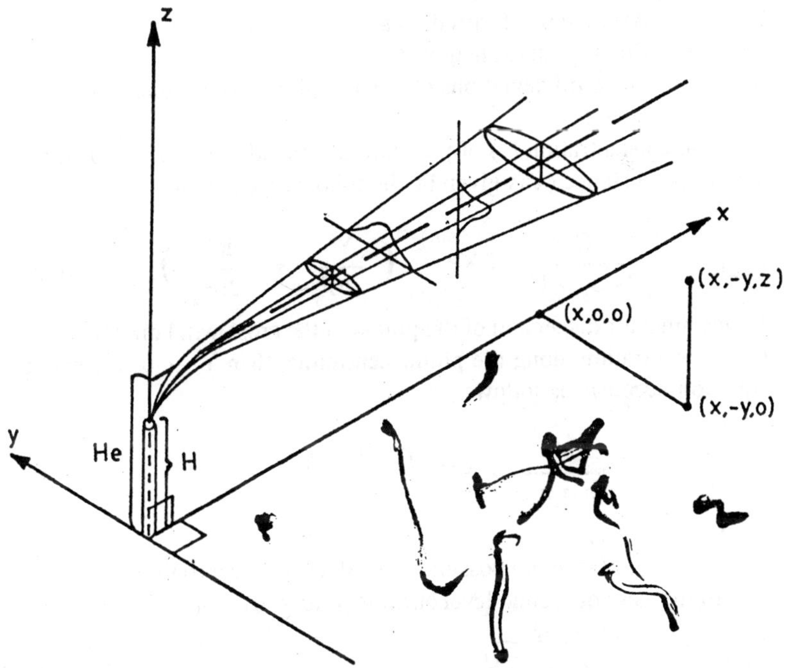

Fig. 6.1. Co-ordinate System showing Gaussian Distributions in the Horizontal and Vertical (after Turner, 1967).

The Gaussian dispersion model equation is as follows.

$$C_{x,y,z,He} = \frac{Q}{2\pi\sigma_y\sigma_z U}\left[EXP-\left(\frac{Y^2}{2\sigma_y^2}\right)\right]\times$$

$$EXP\left\{-\frac{(Z-He)^2}{2\sigma_z^2}\right\}+EXP\left\{-\frac{(Z+He)^2}{2\sigma_z^2}\right\} \quad (6.1)$$

where

C = Concentration of pollutant, g/m^3

Q = Pollutant emission rate, g/s

U = Average wind speed, m/s

He = Effective stack height, m

σ_y, σ_z = Standard deviations of horizontal, vertical plume concentrations

The concentration (c) of pollutant at ground level (Z = 0) for a downward distance (x)is given by the following equation.

$$C_{x,y,o,He} = \frac{Q}{2\pi\sigma_y\sigma_z U}\times EXP-\left(\frac{Y^2}{2\sigma_y^2}+\frac{He^2}{2\sigma_z^2}\right) \quad (6.2)$$

Y^2 accounts for dispersion of the plume in the cross-wind direction. For concentration along the plume centreline, then Y = 0 the above equation becomes as follows.

$$C_{x,o,o,He} = \frac{Q}{2\pi\sigma_y\sigma_z U}\times EXP\left(-\frac{He^2}{2\sigma_z^2}\right) \quad (6.3)$$

where

$C_{x,o,o,He}$ = Maximum possible ground level concentration.

In the case of ground level burning, (He = 0),

$$C_{x,o,o,o} = \frac{Q}{\pi\sigma_y\sigma_z U} \quad (6.4)$$

The important parameters in the Gaussian model are the effective stack height and the variances U_y, U_z for different meteorological conditions which are as follow. Using the Table 6.1 and Fig. 6.2(a) and (b), the variances can be obtained for a specific field condition and maximum possible ground level concentrations can be calculated using equation 6.3. The Gaussian models usually give reasonable estimates of pollutant concentration levels, but their use is limited to other than light wind or variable conditions.

They should work reasonably well for areas with constant surface roughness since the variances dependent on them . However, for areas with varying surface roughness, when the Gaussian model cannot satisfy, alternate methods must be found. The advantage of the Gaussian model is that a minimum amount of data is required. The disadvantage is that the model fails to describe reality of the terrain (in practice, the terrain is not uniform).

Table 6.1. Atmospheric stability classifications

Surface wind speed m/s	Day Solar insolation			Night Cloudiness	
	Strong	Moderate	Slight	Cloudy	Clear
col.1	col.2	col.3	col.4	col.5	col.6
<2	A	A–B	B	E	F
2–3	A–B	B	C	E	F
3–5	B	B–C	C	D	E
5–6	C	C–D	D	D	D
>6	C	D	D	D	D

col.1 = Surface wind is measured at 10 m above the ground.
col.2 = It corresponds to clear summer day with sun higher than 60° above the horizon.
col.3 = It corresponds to a summer day with as few broken clouds, or a clear day with 35–60° above the horizon
col.4 = It corresponds to a fall afternoon of a cloudy summer day, or clear summer day with the sun 15–35° above the horizon.
col.5 & = Cloudiness is defined as the fraction of sky
col.6 = Covered by clouds

For A–B, B–C, C–D conditions, average the values obtained for each. A = Very unstable, B = Moderately unstable, C = Slightly unstable, D = Neutral, E = Slightly stable, F = Stable. Regardless of wind speed, class D should be assumed for overcast conditions, day or night.
(source: Turner, 1970)

Worked out example

Estimate the plume centre line concentration of sulphur dioxide which is released from a power plant, by burning of 10,000 tons of 1% sulphur coal per a day. The stack height is 250 m. The average wind speed at 10 m above ground level is 3 m/s. The variance (hourly mean) values are as follows.

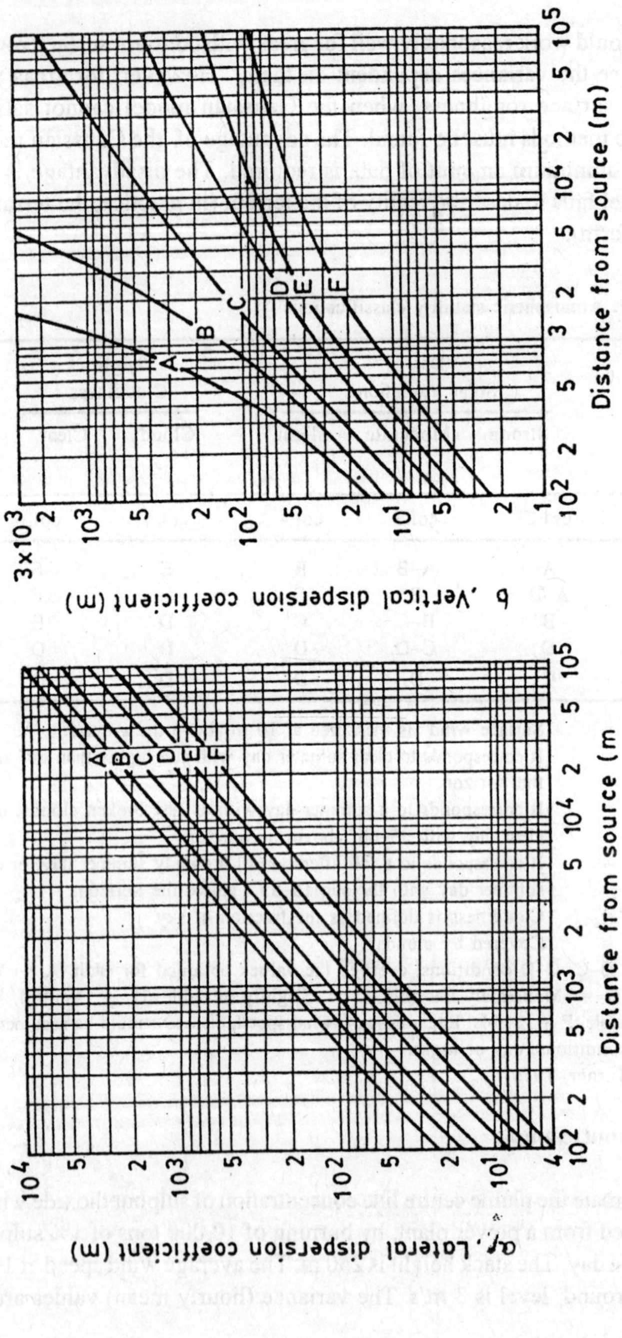

σ_y, Lateral dispersion coefficient (m)
Distance from source (m
(a)
A
B
C
D
E
F
б ,Vertical dispersion coefficient (m)
Distance from source (m)
(b)
A
B
C
D
E
F

Fig. 6.2(a) and(b).

The atmospheric condition is unstable

Solution

Wind speed at 250 m height is calculated based on power law.

$U = U_1 \times (z/z_1)^{0.25}$, where n = 0.25

$= 3 \times (250/1)^{0.25} = 6.6$ m/s

Distance (x) km	σ_y m	σ_z m
1	140	125
5	540	500

To calculate plume center line concentrations.

$$C_{x,0,0,He} = \frac{Q}{\pi \sigma_y \sigma_z U^2} \times EXP\left(\frac{He^2}{2\sigma_z^2}\right)$$

The emission rate of pollutant (Q) is calculated as follows.
Assume all sulphur goes up to the stack and sulphur content in burning total coal is,

$$\text{Total sulphur (g/s)} = \frac{10{,}000 \times 10^6}{24 \times 60 \times 60} \times \frac{1}{100} = 1157.4$$

Total sulphurdioxide produced:

S	+	O_2	=	SO_2
32		32	=	64

Hence sulphur dioxide produced = Two times the total sulphur
= 1157.4 × 2 = 2314.8 g/s

The centre line concentration at x = 1 km:

$$C_{1,0,0,250} = \frac{2314.8 \times 10^6}{3.14 \times 140 \times 125 \times 6.6} \exp - (250^2/2 \times 125^2)$$

= 863.36 micrograms per cubic meter

$$C_{5,0,0,250} = \frac{2314.8 \times 10^6}{3.14 \times 540 \times 500 \times 6.6} \exp - (250^2/2 \times 500)^2$$

= 364.77 micrograms per cubic meter.

Estimate the ground concentrations of oxides of nitrogen at 1 km downward. The wind velocity is 4 m/s and variance values in y and z direction at neutral condition is 70 m and 50 m respectively. The emission rate is 3 g/s.

Solution

$C_{x,0,0,0}$ = Maximum possible ground level concentration.

In the case of ground level burning, (He = 0),

$$C_{x,0,0,0} = \frac{Q}{\pi \sigma_y \sigma_z U}$$

$$C_{1,0,0,0} = 3 \times 1000000/(3.14 \times 70 \times 50 \times 4)$$

$$= 68.20 \text{ micrograms per cubic meter.}$$

The emission rate of a pollutant is 0.01 kg/s, which are releasing from a stack, whose effective stack height is 20 m. The average wind velocity is 4 m/s. Find the maximum ground level concentration at 200 m from the stack. The weather condition is unstable supper adiabatic and corresponding σ_y = 36 m and σ_z = 20 m.

Solution

$$C_{x,0,0,He} = \frac{Q}{\pi_{\sigma y} \sigma_z U} \times \exp\left\{-\frac{He^2}{2\sigma^2_z}\right\}$$

$$= \frac{0.01 \times 10^9}{3.14 \times 36 \times 20 \times 4} \times \exp\left(-\frac{20}{2 \times 400}\right)$$

$$= 669.7 \text{ micrograms per cubic meter.}$$

6.3 PLUME RISE

The plume rise is defined as the difference between the effective stack height (He) and the physical stack height (H).

Plume rise (ΔH) = He – H, or

Effective stack height = Physical stack height + plume rise

$$He = H + \Delta H$$

Hence, plume rise is nothing but the vertical distance between the top of the chimney to the centreline of the plume. It occurs due to buoyancy and momentum of the exhaust gases and also the stability condition of the atmosphere at that time in a particular locality. Buoyancy results when exhaust gases are hotter than the ambient air (atmospheric air) or when the molecular weight of the exhaust gas is lower than that of air or a combination of both. Momentum is caused by the mass and velocity of the exhaust gases. Though plume rise depends on both momentum and buoyancy, generally it is assumed that the exhaust gases have molecular weight which is approximately same as that of air (28.9 g/mole) and hence it may be neglected the buoyancy due to density differences of air and gaseous pollutants. In fact plume rise can increase the effective stack height by a factor of two to ten times the physical height of the stack. Hence, it is an important parameter in determining ground level concentration of the pollutants.

In the literature, numerous empirical formulae are available to calculate plume rise. These empirical models give a definite relationship between various parameters which will influence the plume rise. But, they work under certain assumptions and limitations. Prominent of those formulae are Brigg's, Holland, Lucas-Moore, and Moses-Carson models, etc. which are in Table 6.2.

Table 6.2. Empirical formulae for plume-rise calculations.

Author			Formula
Brigg	ΔH	=	$0.84\ (12.4 + 0.09\ H)\ Q_h^{0.25} / U$
Holland	ΔH	=	$U_s\ d/U\ \{1.5 + (2.68 \times 10^{-3}\ p\ d)\}$
Lucas-Moore	ΔH	=	$135\ Q_h^{0.5} / U$
Moses-carson	ΔH	=	$K_s/U\ (-\ 0.029\ U_s\ d + 5.53\ Q_h^{0.5})$

ΔH = Plume-rise, m
U_s = Stack exit velocity, m/s
d = Inside diameter of stack, m
U = Wind speed, m/s
Q_h = Heat emission rate (k Cal/s)
K_s = Constant for stability, which is 2.65 for unstable. 1.08 for neutral and 0.68 for stable.
p = Atmospheric pressure, 1013 millibars

A suitable formula has to be selected based on local atmospheric conditions.

Worked-out example:

Calculate the effective stack height of a plume which is coming from a 200 m height stack of 1.0 m diameter. The average wind velocity is 3 m/s. Ambient air temperature is 15 °C and barometric pressure is 1050 millibars. The temperature and exit velocity of stack gas are 150 °C and 9 m/s respectively. Use Holland's formula for plume rise calculations.

Solution

Effective stack height = Stack height + plume rise

Stack height = 200 m

Plume rise calculations based on Holland's formula:

$$\Delta H = \frac{U_s d}{U} \times \left\{ 1.5 + \left(2.68 \times 10^{-3}\, p \frac{(T_s - T_a)\, d}{T_s} \right) \right\}$$

where

U_s = Stack gas exit velocity = 9 m/s

d = Diameter of stack = 1.0 m

U = Wind velocity = 3 m/s

p = Atmospheric pressure in millibars = 1050

T_a = Air temperature = 273 + 10 = 283 °K

T_s = Stack gas temperature = 273 + 150 = 423 °K

$$\Delta H = \frac{9 \times 1.0}{3} \times \left\{ 1.5 + \left(2.68 \times 10^{-3} \times 1050 \frac{(423 - 283)1.0}{423} \right) \right\}$$

$$= 7.3 \text{ m}$$

Effective stack height = 200 + 7.3 = 207.3 m

CHAPTER 7

Pollution Control Methods

7.1 PARTICULATE POLLUTION CONTROL METHODS

Methods of removal of particulate matter may be classified into five types. They are as follows:

(i) Setting chambers
(ii) Cyclone separators
(iii) Wet collectors (scrubbers)
(iv) Bag filters, and
(v) Electro Static Precipitators (ESP)

(i) Settling Chambers

They are closed tanks having inlet and outlet arrangements. The polluted gas is allowed to enter into the chambers, where the velocity of the gas is reduced sufficiently to minimise the turbulence nearer to the laminar flow condition, which will allow the particulates to settle by gravity and separates from the gas stream. To ensure uniform velocity, baffle or mesh screens may be suspended in the chamber. A hopper bottom with 1:1 slope is provided at the bottom of the setting zone to collect the settled particulate matter. The flow velocity is usually in the range of 0.5 to 3 m/s. The minimum size of particle which can be removed is 10 micron. Efficiency is high for the removal of particles greater than or equal to 50 microns.

Advantages:

(a) Simple in construction
(b) Low initial cost and low maintenance cost
(c) Dry and continuous disposal of solid particles is possible
(d) Low pressure drop

(e) Efficiency is high for coarse particles
(f) No moving parts involved

Disadvantages:

(a) More space is required
(b) Efficiency is less for low concentration suspensions and lesser sizes of particles
(c) Laminar conditions may not exist always

Design of Settling Chambers

The design of settling chambers for particulate air pollutant is same as the gravitational settling of particles in a fluid. The principle involved is that the velocity of incoming gas is reduced in the chamber by some arrangement (providing baffles, etc), so that the in the gas stream are made to settle by gravity. Hence, settling velocity of particles in the settling chamber has to be estimated. Based on assumptions, a formula can be derived for calculating the minimum diameter of a particle that can be removed with 100% efficiency. To derive the formula, consider a settling chamber which allows a polluted gas (containing particles) and leave after a finite period of time, as shown in Fig. 7.1.

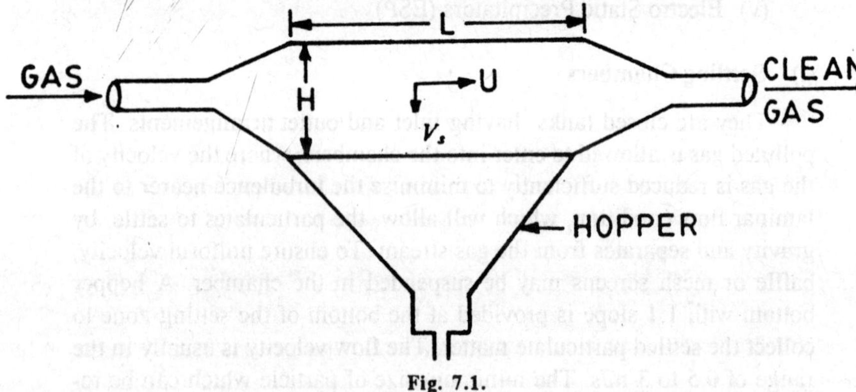

Fig. 7.1.

where

Q	=	Flow rate of polluted gas
L	=	Length of the chamber
H	=	Depth of the chamber
U	=	Horizontal velocity component of the gas
v_s	=	Settling velocity of particles
d	=	Diameter of a particle

The reduction of velocity of gas is done to such an extent that it gives laminar flow condition in the settling chamber. Under this condition, the time required for the gas to travel from inlet to outlet is,

$$t = L/U$$

similarly, the settling velocity of a discrete particle is defined as,

$$v_s = H/t \text{ or } t = H/v_s$$

Hence, $L/U = H/v_s$

$$v_s = HU/L \quad (7.1)$$

Under laminar conditions, the settling of a discrete particle is estimated by Stroke's law, which is as follows.

$$v_s = g\,(S_{s.p} - 1)\, d_p^2 / (18\, v_a) \quad (7.2)$$

where

$S_{s.p}$ = Specific gravity of the particles

v_a = Kinematic viscosity of the polluted air, which is a function of the temperature of the polluted air.

Equate equations (7.1) and (7.2),

$$H\,U/L = g\,(S_{sp} - 1)\, d_p^2 / (18\, va)$$

Rearrange the terms for d_p,

$$d_p = \left\{\frac{H\,U\,18}{L\,g} \cdot \frac{v_a}{S_{s.p.} - 1}\right\}^{0.5} \quad (7.3)$$

$$d_p = \left\{\frac{H\,U}{L\,g} \cdot \frac{18\,\eta_a\,\rho_a}{\rho_a\,(\rho_p - \rho_a)}\right\}^{0.5} \quad (7.4)$$

$$d_p = \left\{\frac{H\,U}{L\,g} \cdot \frac{18\,\eta_a}{(\rho_p - \rho_a)}\right\}^{0.5} \quad (7.5)$$

The equation (7.5) is simplified by neglecting the density of air compared to density of particles, (i.e.) $\rho_p >> \rho_a$; hence,

$$d_p = \left[\frac{18}{g}\,\frac{H\,U\,\eta_a}{L\,g\,\rho_p}\right]^{0.5} \quad (7.6)$$

from eqn. (7.6), the minimum diameter of the particle that will be removed with 100% efficiency in a settling chamber can be calculated.

Worked-out example:

p7.1 Calculate the minimum size of the particle that has to be removed with 100% efficiency. The horizontal velocity of gas is 0.3 m/s. The temperature of gas is 75 °C. The dynamic viscosity of gas is

2.1×10^{-5} kg/m.s. The density of particles is 2000 kg/m³. Length and height of the chamber is 6.0 m and 2.0 m.

Solution:

Use the eqn. (7.6),

$$d_p = \left[\frac{18\ H U \eta_a}{g\ L\ \rho_p}\right]^{0.5}$$

$$= \left[\frac{18 \times 2 \times 0.3 \times 2.1 \times 10^{-5}}{9.81 \times 6 \times 2000}\right]^{0.5}$$

$$= 98.6 \text{ micrometers.}$$

(ii) Cyclone Separators

A cyclone separator is an enclosed vertically placed cylinder with an inverted cone at the base. The inlet is arranged with a tangential entry and an outlet arrangement at the top of the cylinder. This is shown in Fig.7.2. The particulate containing gas enters the cylinder through the tangential inlet which gives a whirl motion. The polluted gas pushes towards the periphery of the cylinder. Due to centrifugal action, the heavy particles move towards the edge of the cyclone. There, the particles slide down into a conical collector (hopper bottom). The gas further proceeds downward and reaches the bottom of the conical section. There the gas moves upwards as a small inner spiral (due to cone base), which is concentric to the first spiral. After reaching the top of the cylinder, the clean gas leaves the cylinder through an outlet pipe.

Advantages:

(a) It is simple in construction and design.
(b) Low initial cost and low maintenance cost.
(c) No moving parts.
(d) Pressure drop is less (25 mm to 200 mm).
(e) It can be constructed with different types materials to meet high temperature and pressure.
(f) Dry and continuous disposal of solid particles is possible in the size range of 5 to 40 microns.

Disadvantages:

(a) Equipment may be subjected to abrasion
(b) Low efficiency for particles of size range 5 to 10 microns.
(c) Low efficiency for low concentration suspensions.

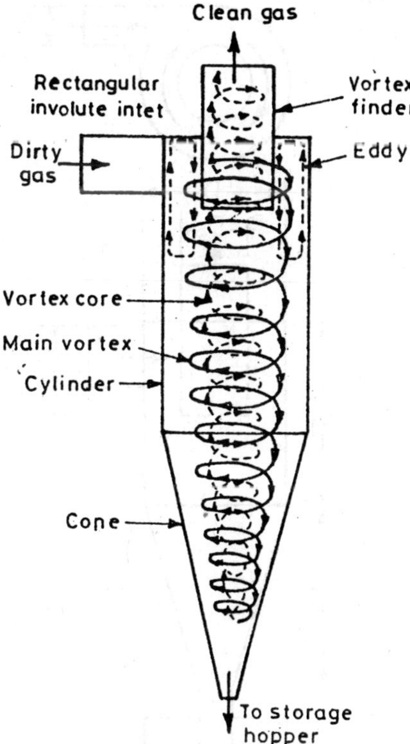

Fig. 7.2.

Design of Cyclone Separator

The separation of particles in a cyclone depends on the magnitude of the centrifugal force exerted on the particles. The separating efficiency is more if the centrifugal force is more. The magnitude of contriugal force is the product of particulate mass and centrifugal acceleration.

$$F_c = M_p \times (U_p^2 / R) \quad (7.7)$$

where

F_c = Centrifugal force
M_p = Mass of a particle
U_p = Particle velocity
R = Radius of the cyclone

If R is less, F_c will be more and collection efficiency is more. This is valid upto certain proportion. Hence, relative dimensions have been fixed for the design, which are shown in Fig. 7.3.

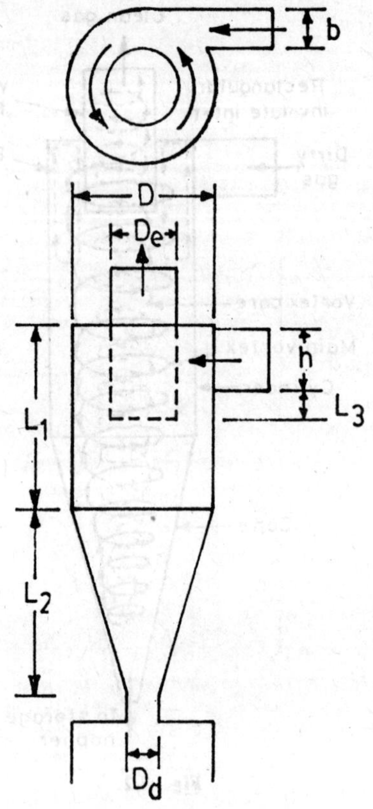

Fig. 7.3.

Length of the cylinder, L_1	=	2 D
Length of cone, L_2	=	2 D
Diameter of exit, D_e	=	0.5 D
Height of entrance, h	=	0.5 D
Width of entrance, b	=	0.25 D
Diameter of dust exit, D_d	=	0.25 D
Length of exit duct, L_3	=	0.125 D

Lapple (1951) has given an equation to find d_{50}, which is given below.

$$d_{50} = \{9\eta_a b/(2\pi\ N_e\ U_i\ \rho_p)\}^{0.5} \quad (7.8)$$

where

d_{50} = Diameter of particle at 50% efficiency, m

η_a = Dynamatic viscosity of polluted air, kg /m/s

b	=	Width of cyclone inlet, m
N_e	=	Number of effective turns with in the cyclone
U_i	=	Inlet gas velocity, m/s
ρ_p	=	Density of the particulate matter, kg/m^3

By knowing the d_{50} size, the relative size ratio, d/d_{50} can be calculated and the efficiency of a cyclone separator is estimated from the graph of efficiency versus relative size, which is shown in Fig. 7.4.

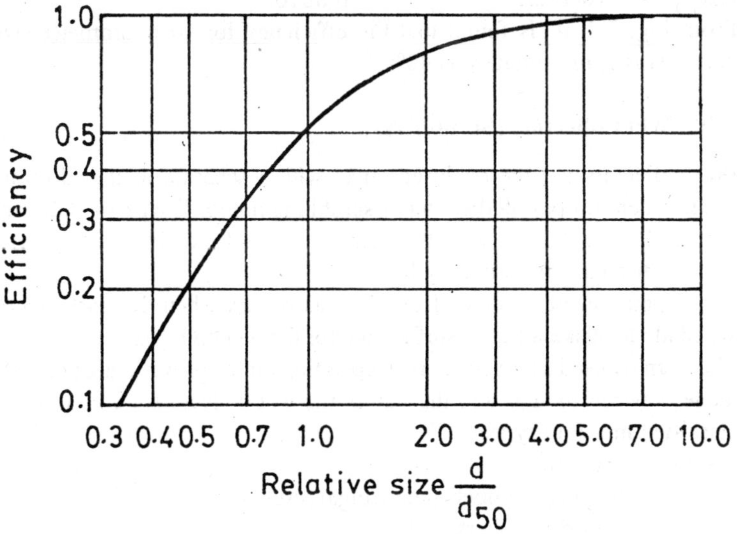

Fig. 7.4.

p7.2 A polluted gas of flow of 8 cubic meter per second is passed through a cyclone separator. The diameter is 2.4 m. It is made with standard proportions. Number of turns is 6 and dynamic viscosity of gas is 1.8×10^{-5} kg/m/s. The size and density of particles to be removed is 10 micrometers and 1.8 g/cm^3 respectively. Find the efficiency of cyclone separator ?

Solution:

To read the efficiency of cyclone separator from the Fig. 7.4 it is necessary to calculate relative size ratio (i.e.: d/d_{50}). Since d is given, d_{50} has to be calculated from eqn. (7.8).

d_{50} = $\{9\,\eta_a . b/(2\,\pi\, N_e\, U_i\, \rho_p)\}^{0.5}$

b = $d/4$ = $2.4/4$ = 0.6 m

h = height of entrance = $2.4/2$ = 1.2

Cross-sectional area of inlet = bh = 0.6×1.2

= 0.72 m^2

$U_i = Q/A = 8/0.72 = 11.11$ m/s

$N_e = 6$

Density of gas $= 1.8$ g/cm³ $= 1800$ kg/m³

$$d_{50} = \left(\frac{9 \times 1.8 \times 10^{-5} \times 0.60}{2\ \pi \times 11.11 \times 1800}\right)^{0.5}$$

$$= 1.135 \times 10^{-5} \text{m} = 11.35\ \mu\text{m}$$

$d/d_{50} = 10/11.35 = 0.8810$

From Fig. 7.4, it is found that the efficiency for 10 micrometer size particles is approximately is 40%.

(iii) Wet Collectors (Scrubbers)

Wet collectors are the enclosed tanks with a separate inlet and outlet arrangement for polluted gas and a scrubbing liquid. The particulates are removed from the gas with the help of a liquid (scrubber). Generally water is used as the scrubbing liquid.

Separation of particles from the gas occurs when the particulates are made to strike a liquid surface within the wet collector.

They can be used as precleaners. Depending on the provisions of contact made between the gas and the liquid, the wet collectors are commonly classified into four types.

(a) Spray towers
(b) Cyclone scrubbers (centrifugal scrubbers)
(c) Venturi scrubbers, and
(d) Packed bed or floating bed towers.

(a) Spray towers: This is shown in Fig. 7.5. Generally the shape is either circular or rectangular and the particles of size range 1 to 2 microns are collected mainly by impingement. The efficiency is 94 to 99% for the size range of 5 to 25 microns.

(b) Cyclone scrubbers: These are similar to the dry cyclone separators. Additionally it contains scrubbing spray system with inlet and outlet arrangement, which is shown in Fig. 7.6. Water sprays are introduced in a variety of ways and the particles are collected by impingement and centrifugal action. It is effective for the removal of 1–2 micron size particles. The efficiency is 90 to 98% for the size range of 5 to 50 microns.

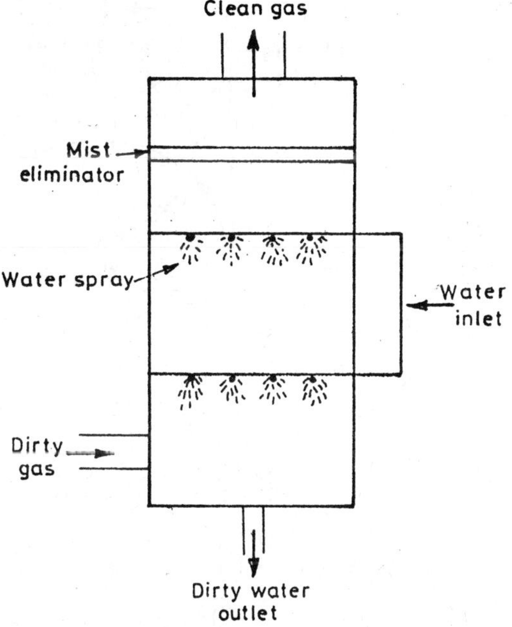

Fig. 7.5.

Advantages:

(i) Low initial cost
(ii) High efficiencies for small particles
(iii) No particle reentrainment
(iv) It can remove the particulates and gas simultaneously.

Disadvantages:

(i) Waste disposal problems
(ii) High power consumption for high efficiency.

(c) Venturi scrubber: It is a wet collector with a venturimeter shape. The gas is introduced through a venturi tube at throat velocity of 60 to 100 m/s. The scrubbing liquid (water) sprays at just ahead of the venturi throat. The particulates are collected along with the falling water. This is shown in Fig. 7.7.

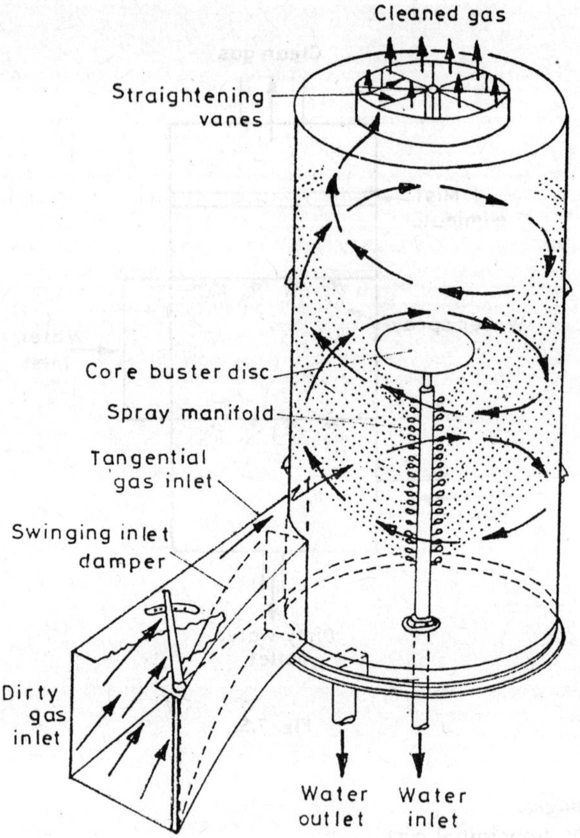

Fig. 7.6.

Advantages:

(i) High efficiency for small particles

(ii) Where cleaning is difficult, this can be used due to compactness.

Disadvantages:

(i) High pressure drop

(ii) Skilled personnel required for design and operation.

(d) Packed bed towers: It is similar to spray tower with an additional facility for a packed bed which is placed at height in a cylindrical tank. The inlet gas is allowed to pass through the bottom of the bed and while passing, an intimate contact between polluted gas and bed occurs. When the gas and particles reaches the top of the bed the

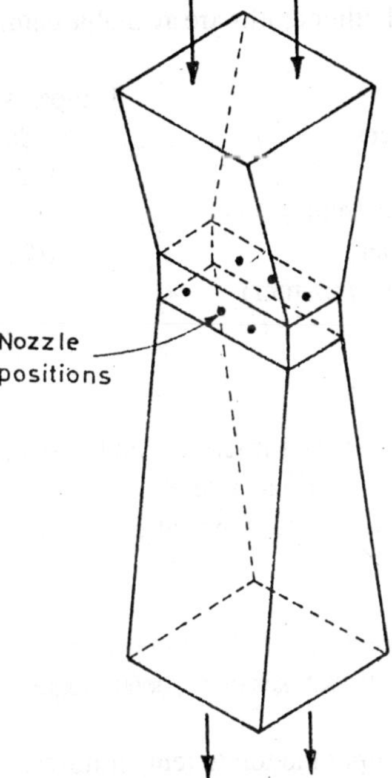

Fig. 7.7.

spray of liquid will catch the particles and carried away along with wash water. The size of particles are removed in the size of particles from 0.2 to 10 microns. The particulates and the gases are removed simultaneously.

(iv) Bag filters

Bag filters are used for the removal of particles of size range of less than 10 microns. These are reliable, efficient system for particulate removals. These are arranged in an encloser called as 'bag house'. The size of each bag is 120 to 400 m in diameter and 2 to 10 m long which are suspended. The outlet ends of the bags are open alternatively and attached to a manifold. The polluted gas enters through the inlet pipe. The large particles will fall into hopper by gravity. The gas flow into the bags and leaves through the outlet pipe. The particulate matter retained on the inside of the bag and form a cake. The cake will be cleaned with the help of the shaking mechanism, causing the filter cake to be loosened. This loosened cake will fall into the hopper which is provided at the bottom of the bag house.

A wide variety of filter cloths are available commercially, which are given below.

Material	Temperature range, °C
Cotton (cellulose fiber)	80 – 85
Wool (animal fiber)	90 –95
Nylon (Synthetic polyamide)	100 – 105
Darcon (poly ester fiber)	125 – 135
Fibre glass (Inorganic polymer)	>250
Teflon	>250

Advantages:

(i) Particles of even 0.01 microns can be effectively removed (high efficiency for small particles)

(ii) Disposal of collected material is done in dry condition

Disadvantages:

(i) High pressure drop and high maintenance cost

(ii) Clogging of filters takes place, hence required freauent cleaning

(iii) Filters work upto moderate temperatures.

(v) Electro Static Precipitators

Electrostatic precipitators are widely popular for the removal of very small size particulate matte. The polluted gas is allowed to pass between two electrodes as shown in Fig. 7.8. One is a negative charged high voltage electrode (e.g. : wire) and the other is positively charged plate or a cylinder. High potential difference (25 to 100 kv) is maintained between,them. Because of high potential difference, a powerful ionising field is formed. This creates an active glow zone (blue electric discharge) very close to the negative electrode, which is called as CORONA. As the negative ions migrate towards the collecting electrode (low potential electrode),they also charge the passing particulates. The electric field attract the particulates towards the collecting electrode (plate) and deposited there.

Advantages:

(i) High collecting efficiency (99 % +)

(ii) Low pressure drop comparing with high efficiencies

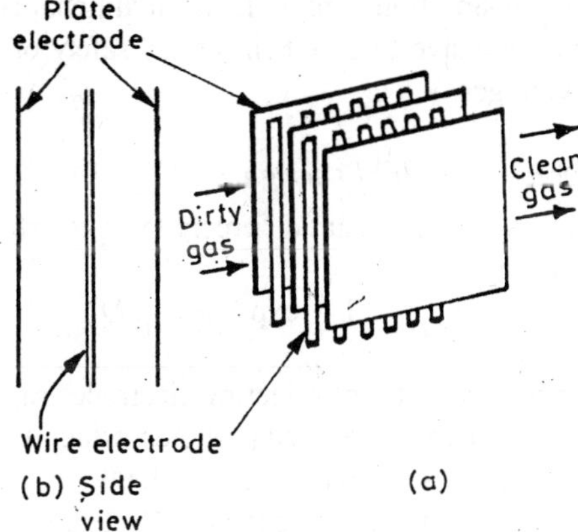

Fig. 7.8(a) and (b).

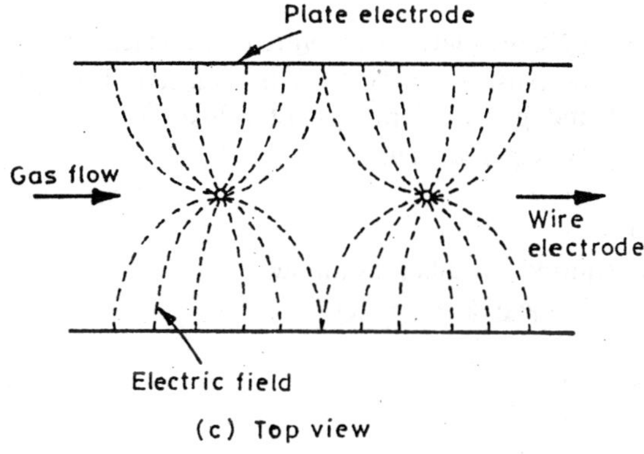

Fig. 7.8(c).

(iii) Very small particles even less than 0.01 microns can be removed
(iv) It can handle the large volume of high temperature gas, and
(v) Treatment time is 1 to 10 seconds
(vi) Wet and dry particles can be collected.

Disadvantages:

(i) Relatively high initial cost
(ii) Skilled personnel are required for the design operation and maintenance
(iii) Ionisation of gas occurs only in a limited operating range Fluctuations drastically reduce efficiency

(iv) Power consumption is more hence maintenance is costly and
(v) Precautions have to be taken for the safety of personnel from high voltages.

Electro static precipitator (ESP) design:

The efficiency of electrostatic precipitator is estimated from the following equation;

$$E = 1 - \exp(-A_s\, v_d / Q)$$

where

A_s = Surface area of the collecting electrodes say plates
v_d = Drift velocity of charged particles, which is defined
= $K \cdot d_p$, (K is a constant, say 300000)
d_p = Diameter of the particle to be collected, m
Q = Gas flow rate, m^3/s

Worked Example

p7.3 Calculate the plate area required for an electrostatic precipitator to remove the particles of size 0.3 micrometer. The system constant is 300000 and gas flow rate is 12 m^3/s.
The efficiency required is 95%.

Solution

The required formula is as follows.

$$E = 1 - \exp(-A_s \cdot \upsilon_d / Q)$$

where

E = 0.95
Q = 12 m^3/s

$v_d = K\, d_p = 3{,}00{,}000 \times 3 \times 10^{-7} = 0.09$ m/s
$0.95 = 1 - \exp -(A_s \times 0.0075)$
$0.05 = \exp(-A_s \times 0.0075)$
$\text{Log}\, 0.05 = -A_s \times 0.0075$
$A_s = 398.97$ say 400 m^2
Area of the plates required for 95% efficiency = 400 m^2

7.2 GASEOUS POLLUTION CONTROL METHODS

Gaseous pollution control methods are classified into three types. They are as follows:

(i) Absorption towers
(ii) Adsorption towers and
(iii) Combustion

(i) and (ii) Absorption and Adsorption Towers

Absorption and adsorption towers may be of two types. One is spray towers and other one is packed bed towers. They are enclosed towers with inlet and outlet arrangements for both polluted gas and sorbing liquid (Scrubber). The polluted gas is sent to the tower through inlet. The gas is made to intimate contact with the spray of scrubbing liquid as shown in Fig. 7.5. The liquid absorbs one or more gaseous pollutants from polluted gas. The efficiency of this process depends on the following factors.

(i) The amount of surface contact between gas and liquid
(ii) Contact time
(iii) Concentration of the absorbing medium, and
(iv) Rate or reaction between the liquid and gases.

Table 7.1 gives the different types of absorbents and adsorbents for various gaseous pollutants.

(iii) Combustion

If exhaust gases are organic in nature combustion processes like flame combustion (furnace) or catalytic combustion (flare) are used. Proper proportion of oxygen, temperature, time and turbulence are necessary for complete combustion.

Flame combustion are of two types.

Incinerators: These are used for the combustible gases to develop a flame in the presence of proper amount of air.

After-burners: These are used for complete combustion of the incinerators effluent gas. Its operation cost is more and removes only combustibles.

Catalytic Combustion: This method is used for the combustion of gases whose combustibility is below flammable range and also the gases having low operating temperature. e.g. : effluent gases from refineries, paints etc. These require high initial cost and catalysts subjected to poisoning. Furnace combustion may be used to control methyl mercaptan, hydrogen sulphide and methyl sulphide odours from kraft paper mill, vapour control from paints and varnishes.

Table 7.1. Absorbents and Adsorbents for Gaseous pollutants

Pollutant	Absorbent	Adsorbent
1. SO_2	Water (Non-reactive) $Ca(OH)_2$ (reactive)	Aluminium oxides + sodium oxides
2. H_2S	NaOH, Soda ash	Iron oxide
3. Oxide of nitrogen	Water, aqueous HNO_3, Urea	Silica gel
4. HF	Water, NaOH	Porous sodium fluoride pellets
5. Nitrogen gas	H_2SO_4	
6. Chlorine	NaOH	
7. Phenol	Chlorine	
8. Aldehyde	Na_2SO_3	
9. Organic vapour		Activated carbon

SHORT/FILL UP THE BLANK TYPE QUESTIONS

1. *Adsorption* is the capture and retention of a component from the gas phase by the surface of adsorbing solid.
2. Absorption efficiency depends on (i) the amount of surface contact between the gas and the liquid, (ii) contact time between the gas and the liquid, (iii) the concentration of the absorption media and (iv) speed of reaction between the *absorbent and the gas*.
3. *Reactive absorbents* are the absorbents which undergo chemical change to remove pollutants (e.g. : water).
4. *Non-reactive absorbents* mean that they will not undergo chemical change and the gaseous pollutants are removed by simply dissolving the gas.
5. *Non-regenerative* absorbent is an absorbent that cannot be regenerated for reuse and must be discarded. e.g. : water + gas ——> water with gas (waste–water).
6. *Regenerative* absorbents means the absorbent which can be regenerated by reversible chemical reaction under temperature and pressure by removing the absorbed polluted gas and regain its original properties.
7. *After burners* are used to effect complete combustion of the incinerator effluent gas.
8. *Flare combustion* is the process of directly mixing a gas with air to production an open flame.
9. Hydrocarbons, ammonia, hydrogen cyanide or other toxic gases are combustion by *flare combustion*.
10. Platinum alloys, vanadium pentoxide are often used as catalysts in *catalytic combustion*.
11. *Venilla flavour* is injected into a primary clarifier at a sewage treatment plant to reduce odour problems.
12. Removal of odour from fish-meal processing is done by *chemical oxidation* process with oxidants like chlorine.
13. Particulates of 1 to 10 microns do bot settle by gravity and they can not be sampled by *dust fall collector*.

14. *Activated carbon* is used for sampling of odourous gases.
15. After burners are used for burning of combustible *gaseous pollutants.*
16. Mean mixing depth (MMD) in coastal areas (200 km from the shore-line) for thermal power plants of capacity 200 MW is *210* meters
17. MMD for inland areas for power plants of capacity of 200 – 500 MW is *220 m.*
18. MMD for inland areas for power plants of capacity greater than 500 MW is *275* m.
19. Minimum stack height is *30* m.
20. *Absorption* means dissolving of a soluble gas in a liquid.
21. *Electro Static Precipitators* type of air pollution control, device is employed in cement industry.
22. *Scrubber* is an pollution control device that uses a liquid spray to remove pollutants from a gas stream.
23. Stack height of a factory shall be kept at least *two and half times* the height of the tallest building in its immediate neighbourhood.
24. MMD means *mean mixing depth.*
25. *Venturi scrubber* is used to control particulate air pollutants in locations where cleaning is difficult.
26. *Carona* is a blue electric discharge. When an high voltage potential difference is maintained between two electrodes, a powerful ionising field is formed. This creates an active glow zone (blue electric discharge) close to the negative electrode.
27. *Mixing depth* is the height available for the mixing of pollutants.
28. *Teflon or glass fibres* are quite suitable as a filter bag media for gases with temperature in the range of 260–370 °C.
29. Deposite gauges are provided with copper sulphate solution to prevent *growth or algae and weeds.*
30. *0.05% lime* solution is used to absorbs sulphur dioxide.
31. Particles of size less than *one micron* may not settle unless washed down by rain.
32. *Packed bed* scrubbers are used to collect particulates of size 0.5 microns and also to absorb gases.
33. Bag filters are not be used when temperature of the gas is *very high.*
34. Gravitation settling chambers cannot remove particles smaller than *10* microns.
35. *Higher* is the mixing depth, greater is the dispersion of air pollutants.
36. When the particle size is greater than *20* microns, the efficiency of the cyclone increases.
37. Settling chambers can remove particle sizes greater than *1/100* mm.
38. *Carbondioxide, water* is released due to burning of hydrocarbons and carbonmonoxide in after burners.
39. *Wash out* means particulates or gaseous pollutants are collected in rain or mist and settle along with them. This occurs when falling rain drops absorb pollutants. The efficiency depends on the intensity of rainfall and the nature of contaminants.
40. *Rainout* is a another natural atmospheric cleaning process by precipitation. when submicron particles (less than one micron in diameter) serve as condensation nuclei around which, drops or water may form. This occurs within the clouds. This phenomenon increases the rainfall and fog formation in urban areas.
41. Venturi scrubbers are the most efficient in removal of particulate matter of size *less than one micron.*

42. A very important parameter of adsorbents is the ratio is *surface area to volume.*
43. Combustion requires proper proportioning of oxygen *temperature, turbulence and time.*
44. *Activated carbon* is used to adsorb odours caused by mercaptans, sulphides and other organic vapours.
45. Urea is used as a scrubbing liquid for the removal of *oxides of nitrogen.*
46. Water is a *non-reacting* absorbent.
47. The *cyclone separator* is used to collect hot and imflammable dusts.
48. Scrubbers are filled with packing material for increasing the *surface area* of contact between the absorbent and the pollutant.
49. Cyclone and settling chambers are used to remove dust, fly ash, fibres, wood dust and particles of size greater than *ten microns.*
50. The factors which influence adsorption are surface area of adsorbent, adsorbate, temperature and *rate of reaction.*
51. Particles of size greater than *one micron* tend to settle because of their self weight.
52. When the concentration of a pollutant is low, its solubility in the liquid is expressed as

    $P = k_H X$, *where P = Partial pressure of the pollutant and X = mole fraction of the pollutant,*

    k_H = *Henry's constant.*
53. Mechanical collectors remove dust, fly ash, fibres and other particles of size greater than *ten microns.*
54. Particulates of size greater than *ten microns* become fastly settleable due to their size and weight.

CHAPTER 8

Automobile Pollution

8.1 INTRODUCTION

Automobiles are broadly classified into two types

(i) Petrol used vehicles, e.g.: cars, aeroplanes

(ii) Diesel used vehicles, e.g.: buses, lorries, etc.

Petrol used vehicles are further classified into two types

(a) Two stroke petrol vehicles, e.g.: auto rickshaws, motor cycles and scooters, etc.

(b) Four stroke petrol vehicles, e.g.: cars, etc.

Due to urbanisation, the automobile pollution is significant and serious one similar to the other types of pollutions. Automobile exhaust pollution gives line source pollution while it is running, (i.e.) vehicles move on a road and exhaust emission comes out along the moving direction. Hence it is more difficult to control. It gives high levels of pollution in densily populated and built up areas and the pollutants emission is very close to ground level. The exhaust emissions either quantity and quality wise are more health hazard like industrial pollution. The magnitude of problems is ever increasing due to rapid urbanisation and industrialisation. Hence serious attention has to be made for automobile pollution control similar to industrial pollution.

8.2 SOURCES AND TYPES OF POLLUTANTS

The pollution from automobiles originates from three sources.

(a) Exhaust gases

(b) Leakages from crankcase or carburetter

(c) Evaporation from fuel tank

The sources of automobile pollution emit carbonmonxide (CO), unburnt hydrocarbons, oxides of nitrogen, oxides of sulphur, smoke and lead particles, etc. The % variation of these pollutants depends on the fuel used and operating conditions of the vehicles.

The type of pollutants emitted by the diesel or petrol vehicles from the source of pollution are given in Table 8.1.

Table 8.1. Typical pollutants present in exhausts of fuels (g/L).

Petrol	Diesel	Pollutants
291.0	6.0	CO
52.4	18.0	CH_x
11.3	22.2	NO_x
0.9	4.0	SO_2
0.4	1.0	Aldehydes
1.1	11.0	Particulates
White smoke + lead	Black or gray smoke + lead	

(Reference: Air pollution by H.C. Perkins)

From this table, it can be seen that petrol engine emission contain high carbon monoxide, unburnt HC, NO_x, less sulphurdioxide, lead particulates and aldehydes. Diesel engine vehicle emissions contain NO_x high), unburnt HC (relatively high), CO, SO_x and more visible smoke, irritant odours, and aldehydes etc.

Generally diesel vehicles create relatively less pollution problem compared to gasoline. Diesel engine vehicles produce 1/10 of CO produced by petrol engine vehicles. The major problem of diesel engine are smoke and odour. Barium is used as fuel additives to supress the smoke. Isopropyl nitrate is used for supression of white smoke. Phosphorus is used as corrosion inhibitor.

HARTIDGE SMOKE METER is used to measure smoke from exhaust pipe. Permissible level is 70 HSU, (Hartridge Smoke Units). Refer IS: 905, for further details.

8.3 CONTROL METHODS

Approximately 85% of air pollution is contributed by exhaust pipe emission and crankcase leakages. The important exhaust emissions from petrol engine are carbon monoxide, unburnt hydrocarbons, carbon particles, oxides of nitrogen and lead particles. These emissions vary with the air fuel ratio, spark times and the engine operating conditions. To meet the exhaust emission standards for CO and HC, air is injected into the exhaust manifold near the exhaust valves. There the exhaust gas temperature is high, which enables further oxidation of unoxidised or partially oxidised substances. Roughly 60% of HC comes form the exhaust pipe emissions.

Crankcase emissions are controlled by providing a device positive Crankcase Ventilation (PVC). This enables the returning gas to the cylinder to be burned inside the engine instead sent to the atmosphere. Approximately 20% of HC from the leakage of crankcase.

Evaporation emissions are the unburnt hydrocarbons. Generally 20 % of HC comes by evaporation. They can be reduced by providing the fuel tank in another built-in chamber with necessary provision for thermal expansion of fuel.

The autoexhaust pollution can be managed by the following.

(a) Improved designs of automobile engines
(b) Good traffic management
(c) Adoptation of better fuels
(d) Regional and town planning
(e) Good driving practices
(f) Wide roads, green belt and good road maintenance etc.

SHORT/FILL UP THE BLANK TYPE QUESTIONS

1. Additives with a barium content of 1g. per litre of fuel have reduces smoke by *50 to 70 %* but caused a marginal increase in CO levels.
2. Men have greater levels of *lead* in their blood than women, urban residents have greater levels than rural residents and smokers have greater levels than nonsmokers.
3. Lead particles from automobiles is less than *2 microns.*
4. Adults ingest *lead* via food and water about 300 micrograms per day and excrete 30 to 40 micrograms per day.
5. Carbon monoxide concentration in cigarette smoke is approximately in the range of *400 to 450* ppm.
6. The emission of a diesel engine contain 40% more oxides of nitrogen but 39% less *hydrocarbons* compared to the petrol engine.
7. Partial oxidation products of hydrocarbons are like *aldehydes, alcohols, benzo-pyrenes.*
8. Complete burning occurs due to increased air-fuel ration and thereby reduces *CO* and *unburnt HC* to zero levels, but due to rise in temperature NO_x increases.
9. 1 gram of *barium* is added to one litre of petrol as additive to reduce smoke by 50 to 70% but causes marginal increase in *CO* level.
10. *Barium* (1g/1 of fuel) is used as smoke suppressor.
11. Carbon monoxide caused death when the concentration is greater than *750* mg/1.
12. *Hartridge smoke meter* is used to measure the smoke from auto exhausts.

13. *Lead* compounds are used anti-knocking agents in the auto fuels.
14. Ringleman chart is a chart made up to graduated shades of grey that vary by five equal steps between *white* and *black.*
15. As per the EPA (Environmental Protection Agency) data, in U.S.A. pollution contributed by transportation is *42% in 1968, 51% in 1969, and 56% in 1977.*
16. Out of the three primary gaseous pollutants emitted directly from the auto exhaust (CO, HC and NO_x), the most toxic pollutants is *carbon monoxide.*
17. Phosphorous is added to auto fuels as a *corrosion inhibitor.*
18. 85% of air pollution of auto mobiles comes from *tail pipe exhausts.*
19. Diesel engine smoke can be reduced by *proper maintenance of engine*
20 Smoke is more in *diesel* engine emissions than *petrol* engine emissions.
21. Iso propyl nitrate have been used to suppress *white smoke* of petrol engines.
22. The exhaust emissions from diesel engines are *odour, smoke, CO, unburnt hydro-carbons, oxides of nitrogen and noise.*
23. Pollutants in petrol engine exhausts are (give in the order as per the quantity wise) *CO, HC,* NO_x.
24. Pollutants in diesel exhausts are (give in the order as per the quantity wise) smoke, NO_x, *HC, CO.*
25. *Lead oxides* of automobile exhausts causes nervous disorders and burning sensation of feet.
26. Benzene (fuel) gives butadin which leads to *lung cancer.*
27. Lead is found in atmosphere from *antiknocking* compounds of gasoline.
28. *Ringleman's smoke chart* is used to measure the apparent density of smoke.
29. Unlead petrol contain *2 to 3* times more benzene than leaded petrol.
30. The increased incidence of lung cancer in industrial and urban areas is attributed to the rising levels of *benzo-pyrene* from automobile exhausts.
31. Cigarette smoke produces about *0.5* microgram of lead per cigarette.
32. Major particulate pollutants emitted by auto exhausts are *lead and carbon.*
33. Vehicle emission control certificate was first introduced by *CHRYSLER.*
34. As per EPA, lead exceeding *2* microns per cubic meter over a period of three months endanger public health.
35. As per EPA (1974), recommended *2g* of lead/gallon of fuel and 0.01 g phosphorous per gallon as additives, and the effluent gas should not greater than 0.01 g of lead 0.01 g phosphorous.
36. Density of diesel smoke should not greater than *1 of* Ringleman's chart.
37. Large amounts of *CO* (5%) under idle condition and large amounts of NO_x (3000 ppm) under acceleration condition released from petrol engines.
38. The emissions from diesel engines are, odour, smoke, carbon monoxide, unburned hydrocarbons, oxides of nitrogen and *noise.*
39. Smoke from a diesel engine is classified as *black, white, gray, blue.*
40. Black smoke or hot smoke of diesel engine is primarily due to *unburned carbon small particles of 0.5–1.0 microns.*
41. Black smoke can be caused by an *overloading condition* of vehicle (too much fuel is feed to the vehicle.
42. *White of Gray* smoke is the residue of the combustion of fuel drops (vehicle is correct operation).
43. *Blue* smoke indicates unburnt fuel of lubricating oil droplets which usually means maintenance of automobiles is required.
44. *CO and black smoke* is produced during combustion, when the oxygen present is insufficient to oxidize the fuel fully in automobiles.

45. *CO* is a direct function of air fuel ratio of auto vehicles.
46. *HC* emission is function of injection equipment and combustion chamber in automobiles.
47. The most difficult emission control problem for diesel engines is to reduce both *smoke* and *oxides of nitrogen* simultaneously.
48. *CO* is present in small quantities in the exhausts of diesel engine, because excess amount of air is available for combustion.
49. *Oxides of nitrogen* are the most significant in the diesel engine as well as petrol engine.
50. Diesel engine is not very much behind the gasoline engine (petrol) in respect of gaseous pollutant of *oxides of nitrogen.*
51. *Nitric oxides (NO)* is formed within the combustion chamber at the peak combustion temperature in automobiles.
52. When *NO* from auto exhausts exposed to atmosphere, NO_2 and other oxides may be formed.
53. Usually NO_x means mixture of oxides of *nitrogen*, namely *NO* and NO_2.
54. In combustion chamber in auto mobiles, unstable compounds like N_2O, N_2O_3, N_2O_4 and N_2O_5 may decompose spontaneously at ambient conditions to *nitrogen dioxide.*
55. The main causes of smoke formation in automobiles is due to inadequate mixing of the *fuel and air.*
56. Visible emission of diesel engine exhaust are *smoke* and *particulates.*
57. Invisible emissions of diesel engine are CO, unburnt HC, and *oxides of nitrogen.*
58. Unsightliness, smudging character and reduction in visibility is caused by *excessive smoke* and *odour* of diesel engine emissions.
59. The concentration of *CO* correlates with traffic volume.
60. Exposure of high levels of NO_x *ozone, and high humidity* can cause fading of textile dyes, yellowing of white fabric and oxidation of metals.
61. A diesel engine produces more *smoke* for each litre of fuel burnt compared to a petrol engine.
62. In an automobile, the farther, the combustion proceeds towards completion, the less the amount of CO and hydrocarbons emitted, but the greater the amount of oxides of *nitrogen* formed.
63. The gas that is mostly emitted by gasoline run vehicles but of insignificant amounts in diesel exhausts is *CO.*
64. NO_2 absorbs visible light and at 0.25 ppm it reduces visibility.
65. NO_2 gas is responsible for the reduction of visibility of the environment.
66. Unleaded petrol was introduced in *April, 1995,* in major metropolitan cities in India.
67. Name the anti-knocking agent: Noise reduction substances is added to petrol: *Tetra ethyl lead.*
68. Positive crank case ventilation is used to reduce *hydrocarbons* from auto mobiles.
69. From air quality points of view which is better, patrol engine or diesel engine ? *Diesel engine.*
70. What types of pollutants will be presented in an exhaust gas of automobiles ?

    CO, HC, NO_x, (primary pollutants), lead, carbon particulates, fuel additives ⟶boron, manganese and nickel, corrosion inhibitor: phosphorus, Barium ⟶smoke suppressors.

CHAPTER 9

Air Quality Standards and Legislation

9.1 AIR QUALITY STANDARDS

Air quality standards are the statutory values (legally valid) of air pollutants for a specified location and time.

Air quality standards are classified into two types:

(i) Primary standards

(ii) Secondary standards.

Primary standards are the standards sufficiently stringent to protect the public health immediately, which means that these standards must protect even the most sensitive individuals including the elderly and those with respiratory ailments. An "adequate margin of safety" is included to these standards whether they are economically or technologically achievable or not.

Secondary standards are the standards to protect the public welfare (e.g.: plants, animals monuments etc.) from known or anticipated adverse effects. They are meant to be even more stringent than primary-standards. Threshold limits were fixed for some pollutants. A threshold is the pollutant concentration below the point at which none of the receptors experience an ill effect.

Air quality standards define a desired limit on specific pollutant level in the air. This goal includes a long term value for exposure, (e.g.: Annual average concentrations as well as high 24-h concentrations in a year), and also one or more short-term values, (e.g.: 1-h average concentrations in a year). The monitoring of the samples should be uniformly followed over the 12 months of an year with a frequency of not less than once in a week. The sampling period of 8-h for each sample and analysed as per the prescribed procedure.

The first national ambient air quality standards for six pollutants were established. These are given below.

(i) Suspended particulate matter (SPM)
(ii) Sulphur dioxide
(iii) Carbon monoxide
(iv) Photo-chemical oxidants (ozone)
(v) Lead and
(vi) Nitrogen dioxide

These standards were entered in FEDERAL REGISTER, 36, No. 86 of part II of U.S.A. on April 30th, 1971.

As per the "National Ambient Air Quality Standards" of Clean Air Act (1970) of U.S.A., the pollutant exposures covered by air quality criteria are given in Table 9.1.

Table 9.1. National Ambient Air Quality Standards of U.S.A. (Reference: Air Pollution, WHO)

Contaminants	Primary Standards			Secondary Standards		
	μg/m³	ppm	mean	μg/m³	ppm	mean
SPM	75	0.03	a.g.m	60	0.020	a.g.m
	260	0.10	24–h	150	0.060	24–h
SO_2	80	0.03	a.a.m	60	0.020	a.a.m
	365	0.14	24–h	260	0.100	2–h
				1300	0.500	3–h
CO	10,000	9.00	8–h	same as primary		
	40,000	35.00	1–h	- do -		
Oxidants (ozone)	160	0.08	1–h	- do -		
Lead	1.5		3–4 months	- do -		
Nitrogen dioxide	100	0.05	a.a.m	- do -		

Note: a.a.m = annual average mean
a.g.m = annual geometric mean

Emission Standards or Standards of Performance

Emission standards are different from ambient air quality standards. They prescribe the maximum permissible emission levels for given pollutants at their source. These are classified into two types.

(a) National standards applied to new and modified sources.
(b) State standards apply to existing sources.

The emission standards framed by the Central Board for Prevention and Control are given in Table 9.2.

The emission limits prescribed are expressed as concentration of pollutants per unit volume of air under standard of normal conditions, written as Nm^3. The standard conditions means that temperature of air is taken as 25 °C and pressure at 760 mm Hg and zero % moisture.

Table 9.2. Emission Standards

(Ref: Central Board for pollution Control, 1985)

PART - I

1. Cement

Standard for particulate matter emission

Capacity	Protected Area	Other area
200 tpd and less	250 mg/Nm^3	400 mg/Nm^3
Greater than 200 tpd	150 mg/Nm^3	250 mg/Nm^3

2. Thermal Power

(a) Standard for particulate matter emission

Boiler size	Protected area	Other area	
		Old (before 1979)	New (after 1979)
Less than 200 MW	150 mg/Nm^3	600 mg/Nm^3	350 mg/Nm^3
200 MW and above	150 mg/Nm^3		150 mg/Nm^3

(b) Standard for sulphur dioxide control (through stack height)

Boiler size	Stack height
Less than 200 MW	$H = 14 (Q)^{0.3}$
200 MW to less than 500 MW	220 m
500 MW and more	275 m

Q = Sulphur dioxide emission in kg/h

H = Stack height in metres

3. Iron and steel

Standard for particulate matter

Process	Emission limits
Sintering plant	150 mg/Nm^3
Coke oven	–
Blast furnace	–
Steel making–during normal operation	150 mg/Nm^3
During oxygen lancing	400 mg/Nm^3

4. Fertilizer (Urea)
Standard for particulate matter emission

Process	Emission limits
Drilling Tower	50 mg/Nm^3

5. Nitric acid
Standard for oxides of nitrogen

3 kg of NO_x per tonne of weak acid (before concentration) produced.

6. Sulphuric acid
Standard for sulphur dioxide and acid mist emission

Process	Sulphur dioxide emission	Acid mist emission
Single conversion Single absorption	10 kg/tonne of concentrated (100 %) acid produced	50 mg/Nm^3
Double conversion Double absorption	4 kg/tonne of concentrated (100 %) acid produced	50 mg/Nm^3

Guidelines for Minimum Stack Height

1. Plant type — Stack height

For all plants except thermal power plant — 30 m

2. For plants where the sulphur dioxide emission is estimated as Q (Kg/hrs.) the stack height, H in meters is given by

$$H = 14(Q)^{0.3}$$

3. For plants where the particulate matter emission is estimated as Q (tonne/hrs.) the stack height, H in metres is given by

$$H = 74(Q)^{0.27}$$

4. If by using the formula given in 2 or 3 above, the stack height arrived at, is more than 30 m, then the higher stack should be used.

In no case should the height of the stack be less than 30 m.

PART - II

1. Calcium carbide
Standard for particulate matter emission

Source	Emission limit
Kiln	250 mg/Nm^3
Arc furnace	150 mg/Nm^3

(Contd.)

2. Copper, lead and Zinc smelting
   Standard for particulate matter and oxides of sulphur

Concentrator	150 mg/Nm³ for particulate matter
smelter and converter	off-gases must go for H_2SO_4 manufacture. No release of SO_2/SO_3 shali be permitted from the smelter or converter.

3. Carnon Black
   Standard for particulate matter emission

Year of Commissioning	Emission limit
New plants (Built and commissioned after January 1, 1985)	150 mg/Nm³
Existing plants (Built and commissioned before December 31, 1984)	250 mg/Nm³ (till December 31, 1986) 150 mg/Nm³ (from January 1, 1987)

4. Fertilizer (Phosphatic)
   Standard for fluoride and particulate matter

Process	Emission limit
Acidification of rock phosphate	25 mg/Nm³ as total fluoride (F^-)
Granulation, mixing, rock grinding	150 mg/Nm³ of particulate matter from each process

5. Oil Refineries
   Standard for sulphur dioxide

Process	Emission limit
Distillation (atmospheric plus vacuum)	0.25 kg/Te of feed*
Catalytic cracker	2.5 kg/Te of feed
Sulphur recovery unit	120 kg/Te of sulphur in the feed

* Feed indicates the feed for that part of the process under consideration only.

6. Aluminium
   Standard for fluoride and particulate matter

Process	Standard
Calcination	250 mg/Nm³ of particulate
Aluminium smelting	1 kg (F^-)/Te of aluminium produced and 150 mg/Nm³ of particulate matter

9.2 AIR QUALITY LEGISLATION

Some of the air pollution acts of U.S.A. are given below

The first air pollution control act was passed in 1955.

In 1963, CLEAN AIR ACT was passed

In 1965, Amended clean air act was passed

In 1967, Air Quality Act was passed

In 1970, Amended Air Quality Act was passed.

Indian Acts

India was the first country in the world to give the control and prevention of environmental pollution as a constitutional obligation by inserting Article 48-A in the constitution. Article 48-A states "The state endeavour to protect and improve the environment and to safeguard the forests and wild life of the country". Article 58-A also states. It shall be the duty of every citizen of India to protect and improve the natural environment including forests, lakes, rivers, and wild life and to have compassion with living creatures.

In 1986, a new Ministry of Department of Environment and Forests was formed by the Government of India, combining Department of Environment and Department of forests to give an integrated approach about the environmental protection and conservation.

The Air (prevention and control of Pollution) Act was passed in May 16th, 1981 and amended in 1987. In 1986, the Government of India enacted an Umbrella Act called "Environmental Protection Act, 1986. This covers all aspects of environment including noise, air, water and hazardous chemicals etc.

Air pollution Act, 1981 is applicable throughout the country. 'AIR' being a Central Government subject, so the Air Act provides more powers and freedom of action to the Central Board of Prevention and Control of Pollution.

The Amended Air Act 1987 provides important provisions, some of them are as follows.

(i) Air Pollution Act is applicable for all air pollution generating sources.

(ii) 'Noise Pollution' was also cover under this act.

(iii) Establishment of new industries is also brought as statute requirement 'for prior approval' under this Act.

(iv) Powers to closure, prohibition or regulation of industries, including stoppage or regulation of electricity, water or any other services under the directions of the central government.

(v) Penalty has been increased from Rs. 500 to Rs. 10,000 and terms of imprisonment for violation has been enhanced for six months to one year to seven years with fine and for further failure, additional fine at Rs. 5000/- Per day of continued failure.

(vi) Provision is made for any person to serve a Notice against any offence committed under this Act to the Regulatory Agency for action and if Regulatory Agency fails to take action within 60 days, the individual can go to the Court.

Section 16 (2) h of Air Act empowers the Central Board, to lay down standards for ambient air quality without any need to consult the states. Section 17 (1) g of the Air Act provides for laying down the standards for stack emissions by the state Board in consultation with the Central Board.

On the basis of land use and industrialisation, the various areas of a state may be classified into three categories and prescribed the standards. These standards are called as minimum national air quality standards (MINAS) which are given in Table 9.3.

Table 9.3. MINAS (minimum national air quality standards)

Class	Area	Concentration in μg/m³			
		SPM	SO_2	CO	NO_x
A	Industrial and mixed use	500	120	5000	120
B	Residential and rural areas	200	80	2000	80
C	Sensitive areas (Hill resorts, National parks and Mounments)	100	30	1000	30

When monitored throughout a layer of frequency of not less than once a week in a sampling time of 8 hrs., the values shall not be more than 95% of the above.

Table 9.4. Long-term goals of air quality

Pollutant	Annual mean		98% observations below this value	
	μg/m³	ppm	μg/m³	ppm
SPM	40	0.016	120	0.048
SO_2	60	0.020	200	0.060
CO (non-dispersive infra-red method for 8–h)	10000	9	40000	30
Photochemical \oxidants (as ozone by KI method)	60	0.03	120	0.06
	8–h exposure		1–h exposure	

WHO (World Health Organisation) Committee recommended on long-term goals for some pollutants which are given in Table 9.4.

SHORT/FILL UP THE BLANK TYPE QUESTIONS

1. MINAS means *minimum national air quality standards.*
2. *Emission standards* means the standards at the pollution emission sources.
3. Expand L.A.R.: *luminance apparent reflectance.*
4. The silver plate mounted inside the shelter is analysed caused by air pollution as a measure of *reflectance* and is expressed as % of decrease of (tornish of silver plate by air pollution) luminance apparent reflectance.
5. *Air quality standards* means prescribed level of pollutants in the air that cannot be exceeded legally during a specified time in a specified area.
6. Ambient air means the *outside air* or *atmospheric air.*
7. Area source means air pollution generated in an *area.*
8. Environmental Protection Act (EPA) was established on 2nd *December, 1970.*
9. CO ambient air quality standard for 8-h exposure is *5* mg/cubic meter in industria areas.
10. SO_2 ambient air quality standard is *80* micrograms per cubic meter for annual mean in residential areas.
11. NO_x ambient air quality standard is *100* micrograms per cubic meter for annual mean.
12. UNESCO (United Nations Educational, Scientific and Cultural Organisations) conducted a conference on "International Pollution" which was held in *Stockholm, Sweden* in June 1972.
13. In India, on the basis of land use and other factors, the various areas of state may be classified into:
    (A) *Industrial and mixed* (B) *Residential and rural and* (C) *Sensitive areas like hill stations and mounments.*
14. Air Pollution control area means an *area where air pollution is considered to be critical requesting for immediate control.*
15. A protected area is one that is *already polluted being in a metropolitan/industrial location.*
16. Standards for smoke from exhausts of new vehicles is *70* Hartridge smoke units (HSU) and for old vehicles is *60* HSU.
17. A comprehensive law to protect the natural environment as a whole, was brought out in 1986 in the form of the *Environmental Protection Act,* 1986.
18. Permissible limits for CO and SO_2 in an industrial air *5000* and *120* micrograms per cubic meter.
19. Give an example of an area source of air pollution: *Locosheds* or *bus station complexes.*
20. Dust fall rate is monitored by *jar collector* method.
21. Give ambient air quality standard for SPM ($\mu g/m^3$) in industrial area is *500* and residential area is *200.*
22. Air pollution Index, (API) is defined as a number which is obtained by multiplying 100 with the sum of the fractional weighted values of air pollution parameters, with reference to standards.

23. *Primary standard* is the standard sufficiently stringent to protect the public health immediately.
24. In the year *1981* the first air pollution control act was passed and amended in the year *1987.*
25. *Line source* is the source of pollution like a line where pollutants are released from the exhaust pipe of moving motor vehicle.
26. List three air pollutants affecting Visakhapatnam?
    (a) Sulphurdioxide (b) Oxides of nitrogen and (c) Hydrocarbons.
27. Death may occur at *500* ppm of NO.
28. The ambient air quality with reference to SPM in residential zone is *200* $\mu g/m^3$.

CHAPTER 10

Air Pollution Survey and Air Pollution in Indian Cities

10.1 INTRODUCTION

Careful planning is necessary to carry out the air pollution survey. The type of survey to be selected depends on the objectives of the survey. For example, if survey is intended to asses the dust pollution level in a mining area, planning and executing a particulate pollution survey is sufficient. Information regarding the local sources of air pollution, topography, density of population, land use pattern (industrial, commercial, residential, etc.), climatological parameters like wind direction and wind speed, temperature variations, rainfall date, future population predictions, etc. are required to carry out the air pollution survey programme. The general guidelines for planning an air pollution survey in brief are as follows {for details, refer IS: 5182 (part 14)-1985}.

10.2 GUIDELINES FOR AIR SURVEY

The guidelines are as follows.

(i) Selection of sampling procedures including procedures of analysis of air pollutants
(ii) Location of sampling stations
(iii) Period, frequency of sampling and duration of survey
(iv) Method of processing of data, and
(v) Meteorological and other parameters measurements.

(i) Selection of Sampling Methods: In the literature, there may be several methods and instruments available to carry air sampling for various parameters. But, depending on the objectives of the survey, the sampling method has to be selected. For example, the available sampling methods are either in-situ (intermittent or continuous) or remote sensing techniques. Similarly, estimation of concentration of pollutants may be done either by (a) titrimetric, (b) spectrophotometric, (c) selective-ion electrode and so on. The selection of a sampling procedure depends upon the nature of pollutants, required range of pollutant concentration, and conditions prevailing in the sampled area etc.

(ii) Location of Sampling Stations: The location of sampling station is also depends on the objectives of the air pollution survey. The following examples will explain.

(a) If the objectives of survey is to assess for specific purpose, the location of sampling station should be such that it satisfy the requirements. Some of them are given below.

Purpose	Location
Health hazard	Breathing level
Vegetation	Foliage level
Electric wires	At the height of wires

(b) If the objective of survey is to assess for pollution level of an area, the location of station should be in the grid, which may be rectangular or circular. The sampling should be done simultaneously in all the stations in the grid.

(c) If the survey is intended for identifying a particular source of pollution, the sampling station location should be at upwind and downwind of the source of pollution, considering stack height, topographic and meteorological conditions.

For a city of 0.5 to 1.0 million population, the monitoring sampling stations should have 5 to 10 (i.e. : one station for 10 to 20 square kilometers area) and for large cities, one station for 5 to 10 square kilometers is suggested.

For further details, please refer IS : 5182 (part-14)– 1985 (Indian standard for guidelines for planning the sampling of atmosphere and location of monitoring stations). Eigen-vector method and a linear optimization model may be used for designing network for various density of stations. National Environmental Engineering Research Institute

NEERI), Nagpur (India), has established air quality monitoring stations and conducting surveys. A typical survey results has been given in Section 10.3 for parusal.

(iii) Period, Frequency of Sampling and Duration of Survey: The period of sampling means the time period over which a single or a set of samples is collected. The concentration of pollutant is averaged for the this time period. The frequency of sampling means the number of times that the samples are collected during a unit time. For example , the samples may be collected with a sampling period of 3 hours. and a frequency of 8 times a day consecutively or 4 times a day with a 4 h gap between consecutive samples.

The periods and frequency of samples should be such that the data of sampling obtained should be more and also cover over a longer period of time. For example, one 24 hour sample collected once weekly and once monthly respectively will give wrong annual values. If the sampling frequency is not uniform, it is also more unreliable for annual values. It should also taken into account the physico-chemical or biological processes which take place in the atmosphere (i.e., formation or decay of photochemical smog or release of pollen).

Hence, the sampling period and frequency should be prescribed based on statistical methods, to get average concentration of the pollutants.

The duration of sampling means the total time period for which entire sampling programme is carried, say one year (at least one cyclic period). Usually 2 to 3 years data programme is recommended. More the years of the data, more reliable averages can be obtained.

(iv) Method of Data Processing: The sampling data are entered in a prescribed sheet. A typical data sheet of air pollution survey programme is given below.

Data sheet

Location of the sampling station :
Zone : Residential/Commercial/Industrial
Name of the Officer Incharge :
Name of the analyst :
Date and period of sampling :
Temperature, weather :
Wind direction and velocity :

Parameter	sampling time from	to	weight of deposit,	flow rate,	volume of air,	result,
	hours		mg	m^3/min.	m^3	$\mu g/m^3$
Suspended particulate matter						
Filter No. 1						
2						

10.3 AIR POLLUTION IN INDIAN CITIES

10.3.1 Introduction

Air pollution disasters occured in some Indian cities have been reported in the literature of air pollution. The quality of air in urban environment is impaired due to industrial, commercial, constructional activities and vehicular emissions. Hence, assessment of air quality in selected cities in India has necessitated.

In 1978, World Health Organisation (WHO) selected India as the nodal point in South-East Asia for air quality monitoring. The objective of the programme is to alert the governments about the level of pollution in India and other South-East Asian countries. As a part of this programme, in 1978, the air quality monitoring programme has been taken up by the National Environmental Engineering Research (NEERI, Nagpur, India) in selected cities in India.

The ten cities (major urban population cities) namely Ahmedabad, Bombay, Calcutta, Cochin, Delhi, Hyderabad, Jaipur, Kanpur, Madras, and Nagpur has been identified by NEERI to conduct ambient air quality monitoring survey during the year 1978 and 1979. The cities are divided into residential, commercial, mixed and industrial zones based on the activity of the areas. These are given in Table 10.1.

In this programme, the following parameters were measured.

(i) Suspended particulate matter (daily, monthly and yearly averages)
(ii) Sulphur dioxide (–do–)
(iii) Sulphation rate (monthly averages), and
(iv) Dust fall (monthly averages)

The adopted method of measurement of these parameters are as follows.

Table 10.1. Zonal classification of Indian cities for air pollution survey.

(Reference : NEERI)

CITY	Elevation above MSL (m)	Longitude	Latitude	Residential (R)	Commercial (C)	Industrial (I)	Ore area	Mixed
Ahemdabad	55	72°.38'E	2 0°.04'N	L.D.Engg. College	R.C.High School	Shardaban Hospital	–	–
Bombay	15	72°.51'E	19°.01N	Khar colony	U.S.Informaton service	Chembur East	Lal baugh	Chembur (W) I+R
Calcutta	6	88°.20'E	20°.32'N	Bhawanipore	Dalhousi	Cossipore	–	Howrah (I+C)
Cochin	30	76°.14'E	9°.58'N	Compshed kodavantra	PHED sewage pumping station	Udhyog Mandal	–	–
Delhi	216	77°.12'E	28°.35'N	Netaji Nagar	Town hall	Najafgarh	–	–
Hyderabad	545	78°.28'E	17°.27'N	Tarnaka	Abids	Moulali	–	–
Jaipur	390	75°.48'E	26°.49'N	Boju Nagar	Badichawpat	Jhoetwara	–	–
Kanpur	12.60	88°.22'E	26°.26'N	Geo-physics Dept., Kanpur university	Govind Nagar	Lajpat Nagar	–	–
Madras	16	80°.11'E	13°N	Koddam-bakkam	General Hospital	Trivotrivur	–	–
Nagpur	31	79°.03'E	21°N	NEERI premises	Maskasath	MIDC, Hingra	–	–
Visakha-patnam	20	83°.20'E	17°.40'N	Seethammadhara	Jagadamba (central area)	Mindi	(port)	Marri-palenu

Suspended Particulate Matter (SPM): High volume air sampler was used to pass the air through filter paper for 24-h period. Deposited dust was determined gravimetrically and expressed as micrograms per cubic meter of air.

Sulphur dioxide: Sample were collected one to four hour batch basis for a period of 24 hrs. Tetrachloro mecurate solution was used to absorb sulphur dioxide and its concentration was measured colourimetrically and expressed as micrograms per cubic meter of air.

Sulphation rate: It was measured by lead peroxide candle method. Sulphur containing gases were oxidised to sulphate when these gases exposed to candle for a period of one month. The resulting sulphate was estimated gravimetrically or turbidimetry and expressed as milligrams of sulphur trioxide per 100 square centimetres per day.

Dust fall: Dust fall was estimated by using dust fall jar and results were expressed as metric tons per square kilometres per month.

The average results of industrial areas are given in Tables 10.2 and 10.3 (Reference: NEERI).

Even though these values are obselate, but they will give the position of pollution level at that time. It will be useful for comparision of pollution levels in a specified time period.

The data collected for one year and it is not sufficient to get concrete conclusions for long-term effects, but the values give the trend of air pollution by comparing the standards, which are given below.

Suspended particulate matter	=	150 $\mu g/m_3$ for 24-h a.mean
Sulphur dioxide	=	80 $\mu g/m^3$ for a.g.mean
Sulphation rate	=	0.5mg $SO^3/100$ cm^2/day
Dust fall	=	10 metric tons/km^2/month

Similar study on was conducted by NEERI on five selected cities in 1982. The results are given in Table 10.3.

Threat to Taj Mahal : NEERI conducted a air quality survey in July 1993. The pollutants levels at Taj Mahal are as follows.

SPM (suspended particulate matter) 500 $\mu g/m^3$
Sulphur dioxide 50 - do -

Due to the pollutants the pure white marble surface of Taj Mahal turned to a sickly yellow colouration with dark spots. The sources of air pollution in Agra (Uttar Pradesh) are given in Table 10.4.

Table 10.2. Air quality in Indian cities

(Units of parameters are as mentioned in the previous section)
Arithmetic mean values for the 1978.

City	SPM	DF	SO_2	Sulphation rate
Ahemdabad (Shardavben hospital area)	295	91	120	0.24
Bombay (west Chembur area)	243	12	47	0.66
Calcutta (Cossipore area)	353	42	54	0.70
Cochin (Udhyog mandal area)	152	–	106	–
Delhi (Najafgarh area)	431	27	61	0.21
Hyderabad (Moulaii area)	309	56	28	0.13
Jaipur (Jnotwara area)	189	15	09	0.17
Kanpur (Lajpat nagar area)	219	34	20	0.26
Madras (Trivotrivur area)	153	11	27	0.06
Nagpur (Maskasath area)	300	226	06	0.13

Table 10.3. Air quality survey results

City	SPM	SO_2	NO_x
New Delhi			
Summer	350–500	15–20	10–15
Winter	150–200	20–30	15–20
Bombay East Chambur			
Summer	426	36	57
Winter	579	59	115
Calcutta	522	90	–
Bangalore, 1985			
(Amco Batteries)	483.5	91.5	290
Visakhapatnam, 1982-83			
Seethammadhara	322	139(port area)	

Table 10.4. Sources of air pollution in Agra.

Industry	No. of units	Fuel* burnt	Emissions (kg/h) SPM	SO_2	CO
Ferrous casting	131	1,048	3,373	616	70,530
Ferro alloys	34	34	122	20	2,288
Chemicals	34	51	64	85	286
Rubber processing	30	06	08	10	34
Refractory bricks	16	32	36	21	07
Engineering works	20	17	22	29	98
Lime processing	18	59	73	97	329
Total	283	1,247	3,698	878	73,573

* = Million Tons per day; Ref: Current Events, Jan. 1994.

NEERI has regularly monitoring air pollution survey in selected cities in INDIA. The latest reports on air quality are available with them.

CHAPTER 11

Global Air Pollution Problems and Programs

11.1 INTRODUCTION

According to the population census 1991, the population in India is 850 million and the world population is around 5.3 billions. It is inevitable to go for industrialisation to provide minimum needs and to increase the socio-economic status of these populations. Industrialisation increases per capita income of a country and reduces poverty of the people. The Earth's life sustaining environment is expected to change more rapidly due to industrialisation. Hence, it is always desirable that industrialisation should be as sustainable development of man. But, in practice, world wide economic and technological activities are contributing to rapid and potentially stressful changes in the global environment. These changes may profoundly affect generations to come. The most concern is about the fate of the global environment due to increase in concentration of greenhouse gases (carbondioxide, methane and nitrous oxide) and possible effects on the global climate. Since the industrial revolution, the carbondioxide concentrations have increased by 25%. Fossil fuel burning is one of the key processes leading to emissions of greenhouse gases. Industrial chlorofluorocarbons and related gases are also as important as greenhouse gases. The rapid rate of land-use changes that accompany human population growth, especially in the tropics, is contributing to the perturbation of biosphere-atmosphere interactions. For example, the emissions of hydrocarbons, carbonsmonoxide and oxides of nitrogen from biomass burning during the dry season, result in photochemical reactions. Increased rice production contributes methane significantly. Enhanced nitrousoxide release may well result from increased application of nitrogen fertilizers and tropical deforestation activities. These and other anthropogenic (man-made) emissions affect the atmosphere over a range of spatial scales (global). Hence, there is a need to study about global air pollution problems which may be classified as follows.

(i) Green house effect – Global warming and Rise in sea level
(ii) Chlorofluorocarbons (CFCs) - Depletion of Ozone layer
(iii) Acid rain

11.2 GREEN HOUSE EFFECT - GLOBAL WARMING AND RISE IN SEA LEVEL

The atmosphere that surrounds the earth plays a vital role in maintaining normal temperature on the earth's surface. More than 99% of the atmosphere is made up by both nitrogen and oxide. Carbondioxide and other gases are present in smaller amounts.

Solar energy (light rays) from Sun travels in the form of electromagnetic waves as ultra violet, and other short wave radiation and also long wave radiation (Infra red). The ultra violet rays are filtered by the ozone layer and the remaining moves towards the earth's surface. The carbon dioxide present in the atmosphere strongly absorbs radiation in certain long wave infra red portions of the spectrum. The remaining solar radiation in the form of long wave and in the form of short wave are absorbed by the earth's surface and converts to heat energy and emitted into space as long wave radiation. Water vapours and carbondioxide are transparent to short wave radiation and they are nearly opaque to long wave radiation. A small portion of re-radiation long wave radiation passes to atmosphere . The re-radiated long wave radiation passes to atmosphere. The re-radiated wave radiation from the earth's surface again are absorbed by the carbondioxide and re-radiated back to earth's surface. The latter helps to maintain a relatively warm condition between atmosphere and the ground and it thus helps to stabilize temporal variations in the earth's surface temperature, which is most important for plants and animals. Clouds and water vapour in the sky also serve to absorb and emit infra red radiation and contribute to this heating effect. Thus, the atmosphere (mostly carbondioxide) by absorbing of re-radiated long wave radiation of earth acts as a insulation to keep the heat near the surface of the earth. This phenomenon is known as "Green House Effect"

The word "Green House" is nothing but glass house which is constructed to grow tropical plants in cold areas of specific plants in tropical areas. The glass is used as roof cover in a green house which is also transparent to short wave solar radiation and absorb the long wave radiation emitted from inside of the green house and block the re-radiated solar radiation, which maintain the heat sufficient for the plants growth. This is similar to the process of solar short wave radiation reaching the earth's surface and reflects back to the atmosphere from the earth's surface in the form of long wave radiation. The carbon dioxide present in the atmosphere absorbs re-radiated long wave radiation and heat is maintained near the earth's surface sufficient for living world. Hence the latter process is called as "Green House Effect". If more carbon dioxide is present (due to release of Carbon dioxide by fuel combustion) in the atmosphere more heat is retained near the earth's surface.

It has been estimated that carbon dioxide will account for about half of the future temperature increases, while methane, nitrous oxide, ozone and chlorofluorocarbons will be responsible for the rest as shown in Table 11.1.

Green house gases are produces both by industrial and biological processes, but while industrial emissions are fairly well documented. But, the knowledge of the production rates of greenhouse gases through biological processes and the factors regulating emissions is still inadequate. In the next 50 years, the increases in emissions of greenhouse gases to the atmosphere are estimated to result in global warming by 0.3 to 0.5 °C per decade. The increase will not be evenly distributed, the largest increase are expected in northern latitudes during winter. These temperature changes will in turn affect the amount and temporal distribution of precipitation. This may have drastic consequences for forestry and agriculture. Rising temperature will also lead to an increase in the levels of the world oceans due to a thermal expansion and the melting of the Arctic ice cap and glaciers. The increase over the next century is calculated to be 6 cm per decade. The effects on all coastal regions will be drastic.

The carbon dioxide level in the atmosphere is rapidly increasing due to burning of fossil fuels to obtain energy of transportation, electricity and heat generation. Since carbondioxide absorbs infrared radiation, excess heat stays in the atmosphere and rises the mean temperature. If the earth continues to warm-up, all the glaciers and polar ice caps will begin to melt. Many island countries will be submerged, coast line will be flooded due

Table 11.1. Contributions of each of the human-made gases

Contributing gas	Percentage
Carbondioxide	55
Chlorofluorocarbons (CFCs) 11 and 12	17
Methane	15
Other CFCs	7
Nitrous oxide	6

to the rise of sea level by few meter. It is estimated that one-third of the world's population lives within 60 km of the coast line. In the next century, 25% of the world population may be affected by the rise in sea level due to global warming. In the last century, the sea level rose by 10 to 15 cm and by 2050 it is expected to rise further by 23 cm to 116 cm. By 2100 A.D., the rise in sea level may double to 56 cm to as much as 345 cm.

11.2.1 Programs

A major problem is the uncertainty of present forecasts of future climate changes. It is not enough to predict global warming and mean changes in precipitation. It is of the utmost importance to determine the fate of the life support system of the global environment for the next hundred years. The threats are not limited by national boundaries and due to the seriousness of the issues involved, two international research programmes have been launched.

1. In 1986, International Council of Scientific Unions (ICSU), which is a major international non-governmental research organisation launched a programme known as International Geosphere-Biosphere Programme (IGBP). The objective of the IGBP is to describe and understand the interactive, physical, chemical, and biological processes that regulate the total Earth system, the unique environment that it provides for life, the changes that occurring in the system, and the manner in which they are influenced by human activity. The development of a global data and information system that will provide immediate and open access to all researchers. It will provide information needed for Earth system models, and that will define and sustain the long term observations needed to detect significant global changes. Core projects of the IGBP will require the support of many participating nations if they are to be successfully implemented. It is estimated that the core IGBP planning and coordination needs an annual budget of about two million U.S. Dollars. India is one of the participant in this programe.
2. The second programme known as "The World Climate Research Programme (WCRP)", which is jointly sponsored by the world Meteorological Organisation (W.M.O.) and the International Council of Scientific Unions (ICSU). This programme deals with the physical aspects of the climate system and provides a necessary base for the development of predictive capabilities of climate for different time periods.

In India, the Council of Scientific and industrial Research has set up a task force of the National Institute of Oceanography, the National Geophysical Research Institute and the National Physical Laboratory to study the rise in sea level and monitor this closely. Under a UNESCO programme, GLOSS (Global Sea Level Observing System), a network of 297 tide guage stations are to be set up in the world. Of these 50 will be in the Indian Ocean, Mormugao, Veraval, Cochin, Madras, Visakhapatnam, Port Blair, Nicobar and Minicoy are among the places selected already. The existing network is not considered adequate for monitoring sea level rise as the gauges are not sensitive enough.

The east cost with its lower continental slopes and higher frequency of storms will be more vulnerable to the expected rise in sea level as a result of the predicted global warming. Data collected between 1978 and 1985 shows that sea level has been rising at one mm. a year. The task force had identified the areas which would be most vulnerable to a rise in sea level. The Lakshadweep has 27 separate coral reefs and island and most of them are low lying with the highest points not more than a few meters high. The task force has suggested that effect of rise in the sea level would be three-fold. Some areas would get submerged, there would be an increase in storm surges and these could lead to further damage to the coast linc and finally there would be considerable loss of fresh water aquifers because of salt water intrusion.

11.3 CHLOROFLUOROCARBONS(CFCs)-DEPLETION OF OZONE LAYER

The ozone layer of the stratosphere (a part of atmosphere) is present in the atmosphere at altitudes 10-60 km and it is most dense at 20-25 km. The average thickness of this layer is 3 millimeters.

11.3.1 Formation of Ozone Layer in the Atmosphere

Ozone (O_3), a gas composed of three oxygen atoms exists in a dynamic equilibrium in the stratosphere. The oxygen molecules which are produced by photosynthesis, diffused upwards by atmospheric circulation. It is decomposed by ultra violet short wave radiation. The sun emits light over a wide range of wave lengths including infrared visible and ultra violet. The UV radiation which is having high energy damages the skin of man. Fortunately, the high energy UV radiation is removed in the upper atmosphere by a series of photochemical reactions involving molecular oxygen and ozone. Sun light striking an oxygen molecule breaks into two oxygen atoms.

$$O_2 + \text{UV radiation} \longrightarrow (O) + (O) \quad (11.1)$$

The atomic oxygen is highly reactive. Some of the oxygen atoms eventually combine with oxygen molecules and form ozone, which accumulate within the upper atmosphere and acts as filter by absorbing ultra violet radiation.

$$O_2 + (O) \longrightarrow O_3 \quad (11.2)$$

This reaction releases energy, but in the form of infrared rather than ultra violet radiation. If more of the UV radiation that reaches upper atmosphere can penetrate to the surface of the earth, which can cause burns and increases the chances of skin cancer. Thus the biologically harmful high energy ultra violet is converted to infrared radiation and helps to form ozone. The ozone then absorbs additional UV radiation and dissociate as oxygen and nacent oxygen, as given in the following equation.

$$O_3 + \text{UV radiation} \longrightarrow O_2 + (O) \text{ nacent oxygen} \quad (11.3)$$

This nacent oxygen further reacts with ozone and forms as oxygen

$$O_3 + (O) \longrightarrow 2O_2 \quad (11.4)$$

Thus UV radiation is removed by the formation and also the destruction of ozone. The ozone layer is crucial to life on earth since it acts as a ultra violet filter by absorbing much of the ultra violet from solar radiation before it reaches the earth's surface. However this layer may be depleted by reactions involving a variety of compounds which reach the stratosphere.

11.3.2 Depletion of Ozone Layer

Substantial ozone layer losses have appeared over Antarctica, in Northern hemisphere and polar regions. The primary cause for ozone loss is due to increase in concentration in the stratophere of anthropogenic chlorine especially chlorine released by solar UV photolysis from chlorofluoro carbon (CFC) compounds.

Chlorofluorocarbons (CFCs) means CCl_3F (CFC-11), CCl_2F_2 (CFC-12) CCl_2FCClF_2 (CFC-13) etc. After 1930, they became popular in industrial use because of non-toxic, non corrosive, non flammable and thermally efficient properties. These are used in different industries which are given in Table 11.2. As per the US (EPA) estimates of 1986, more than a million tonnes are producing, out of which 43% in Europe and 30% in U.S.A. and while in India is 0.03%.

After use CFCs reach the atmosphere (rise upto stratosphere) as waste gases and even they may stay there in several decades (40 to 150 years). In the lower atmosphere CFCs will not effect the living systems. They are not removed by atmospheric scavenging processess which occurs for sulphurdioxide etc. When exposed to UV radiation in the

Table 11.2. CFCs in Industrial use

CFCs used industry	Percentage
Solvent or cleaning electronic equipments - (CFC-13)	55
Refrigeration Industry and refregerants in air conditioning (CFC-12)	20
Foam blowing agents in Plastic Industry - (CFC-11 or 12)	13.5
Fire extinguishers	10
Aerosol propellants - (CFC-11 + CFC-12)	1.5

stratosphere, they break down and chlorine atoms are released and combine with ozone from ozone layer of stratosphere. Hence ozone layer depletion and formation of holes occurs which allows to pass UV radiation to earth.

11.3.3 Consequences of Ozone Depletion

The primary consequences of Ozone depletion can be described under the categories of climate and biological. The formation of holes and deletion of ozone layer will permit the penetration of ultra violet radiation in to the troposphere, where a number of complex photochemical reactions would occur and generate photochemical smog, etc. It also reduce the forest growth due to failure in pollen germination and damages crop and ecosystems. Biological damages are as follows.

(i) Damage of genetic material and responsible for skin cancer
(ii) Suppressing the efficiency of immune system and making it easier for tumors to take hold and spread
(iii) Increasing the incidence of cataract eye diseases.

Antarctic ozone hole will be an important atmospheric phenomenon throughout the 21st century.

11.3.4 Stratopheric Photolysis of CFC Compounds: (or how CFCs reactions take place or what happens in atmosphere with CFCs).

The relationship between increasing concentrations of the chlorofluorocarbons gases and stratospheric ozone depletion was first outlined by Molina M.J. and Rowland F.S. in 1974. The properties of CFCs are that as follows they are chemically inert and that they can survive unchanged for very long periods even 100 years or more. The physicochemical processes that normally remove trace impurities form the atmosphere-tropospheric sinks such as solar photolysis, rainout or oxidation do not affect the CFCs because they are transparent, insoluble, and chemically unreactive.

Molina-Rowland Theory of Photolysis : The individual CFC molecules diffuse randomly upward into the middle stratosphere and are decomposed by shot wave length solar UV radiation.

$$CCl_2F_2 + UV(<220\text{ nm}) \longrightarrow Cl + CClF_2 \qquad (11.5)$$

These wavelengths of UV radiation do not penetrate sown to the surface of the Earth because they are absorbed in the lower stratosphere wither by molecular oxygen or by ozone. The CL atom released in Eqn. (1) reacts with ozone within a fraction of a second, with the formation of free radical chlorine oxide, ClO.

$$Cl + O_3 \longrightarrow ClO + O_2 \qquad (11.6)$$

The ClO radical can then react within minutes with atomic oxygen and once again releasing Cl.

$$ClO + O \longrightarrow Cl + O_2 \qquad (11.7)$$

The sequence of eqns. (11.6) plus (11.7) constitutes the Clo_x free radical catalytic chain reaction which repeats itself over and over again in the stratosphere before finally being stopped.

$$O + O_3 \longrightarrow O_2 + O_2 \qquad (11.8)$$

The net effect of the two reactions as shown in eqn. (11.8) converts back to molecular oxygen one ozone molecule and one atom of oxygen which would otherwise have formed ozone, making this ClO_x chain an exceptionally efficient method of ozone destruction. The ClO_x chain can be interrupted by reactions with methane and nitrogen dioxide, which form temporary reservoir molecules such as HCl and chlorine nitrate ($ClONO_2$)

$$Cl + CH_4 \longrightarrow HCl + CH_3 \qquad (11.9)$$

$$ClO + NO_2 + M \longrightarrow ClONO_2 + M \qquad (11.10)$$

Stratospheric chlorine can remain chemically inactive in these reservoir molecules for a few hours or days, only to be released once more as Cl by photolysis of $ClONO_2$ or HO reaction with HCl. The average length of the ClO_x chain in the stratosphere before drifting back into the troposphere (Usually as HCl) is about 100,000. The chain of multiplications factor of 10^5 combines with atmospheric release every year of about one million tons of CFCs to make stratospheric ozone depletion by CFCs a major global environmental problem.

Replacements for CFCs in most of their uses are being developed very rapidly and several new compounds from the HCFC and HFC classes are being produced. HCFCs are found efficient as alternatives to all the CFCs. These molecules are different form CFCs because they have C-H bonds that can react with HO in the troposphere.

The reaction is as follows.

$$HO + CHClF_2 \longrightarrow H_2O + CClF_2 \qquad (11.11)$$

This $CHClF_2$ (HCFC-22) is already in wide usage as the refrigerant in all home air conditioners. The other new compounds that will soon be available are HCFC-123 ($CHCl_2CF_3$) for CFC-11 and HFC-134A ($CH2FCF_3$) for CFC-12 in some applications. HCFCs are 10-50% less as ozone depletion potential and 1/3 less as global warming potential.

11.3.5 Programs

An international protocol to control the emissions of CFCs to the atmosphere was agreed in Montreal (Canada) in September 1987. 101 countries signed an agreement called as "Montreal protocol" to reduce CFCs production. Under its terms, the total global emissions of CFCs were to be reduced 20% by 1994 (below 1986 emission levels) and an additional 30% by 1999. This agreement was strengthened at the London meeting in June 1990. However changes were made to modify the technology. In Earth summit meeting held at Rio De Janerio (Brazil) have accepted to complete phase-out by 2000 AD for developed countries and by 2010 A.D. for developing countries. Recent international convention at Copenhagen agreed to phase-out for HCFC by 2030 A.D. Internationally reputed companies like Du Pont stopped manufacturing of CFCs and adopting HCFCs, since it requires minimum changes in design and production.

11.4 ACID RAIN

11.4.1 Introduction

The term "Acid rain" is defined as the rainfall which is more acidic (pH less than 5.6) than the normal natural water.

Generally the acidic characteristic of water is measured by pH, where normal range is 6.5 to 8.5. If the pH of rainfall is less than 6, is considered as acidic. The severe acidic nature of water occurs due to massive air pollution resulted by industrialisation. Hence to avoid acid rain, proper planning is necessary while locating the industries in a region or country.

Due to lack of planning and forecasting about acid rain, several developed countries are facing acid rain problems. Lakes and forests in wet Europe, Canada and U.S.A. and forests in West Germany are affecting due to acid rain. In India also aicid rainfall has been reported in Mumbai (Bombay), Calcutta and Pune. The acid rain not only destructs the lakes and forests, but also it corrodes buildings, monuments, metallic surfaces etc.

11.4.2 Effects of Acid Rain

(i) The acid rain reduce the pH of streams and lakes, which kills aquatic life (fish, etc.) and reduce the growth of plankton and reproduction of fish. Change in pH prevents hatching of fish eggs. Green algae and several types of bacteria which are essential to aquatic life which can not survive in acid environment.

(ii) Acid rain is harmful to forests and vegetation. It causes damage to leaves and accelerates leaf surface erosion. Growth of leaves is suppressed due to high acidity. When growth of leaves are affected and results vanishing of greenery.

(iii) Acidity affects the soil. A plant nutrient such as potassium is gradually leachedout of the soil. Under acidic conditions, toxic metals to plant accumulates in the soil.

(iv) Acid rain also disturbs the microbial acitvity of soil. The microbes in the soil which transforms the organic matter in the soil into nutrients to plants life. When microbial population is reduced as they can not tolerate the acidic environment in the soil due to acid rain.

11.4.3 Causes of Acid Rain

Oxides of sulphur, nitrogen and hydrocarbons are the major contributing factors to acid rain. Huge quantities of oxides of sulphur and nitrogen oxides are emitted into the atmosphere from the chimneys of industrial plants and also from auto exhausts. Burning of fossil fuels for power generation is a major contributor (60-70%) of sulphur dioxide to the atmosphere. Smelting of sulphide ores, particularly of lead, zinc, and copper is also responsible for an increase in the sulphur dioxide content of the atmosphere. The major contributors of oxides of nitrogen are automobile exhaust, power houses and smelters. When these pollutants reacts with moisture and matter already present in the atmosphere forms as secondary pollutants. most of the secondary pollutants resulting from photochemical reactions utilises energy from sunrays.

11.4.4 Nitric Acid Rain Formation

In the atmosphere ultra violet energy is absorbed by nitrogen dioxide and becomes highly energized molecule, then decomposes into nitric oxide and atomic oxygen.

$$NO_2 + h\nu \text{ (solar radiation)} \longrightarrow NO_2 \text{ (energized)} \quad (11.12)$$

$$NO_2 \text{ (energized)} \longrightarrow NO + O \quad (11.13)$$

This atomic oxygen quickly reacts with molecular oxyen to form ozone. If no other energy absorbent molecule is available, ozone decomposes fastly and otherwise a stable ozone molecule is formed.

$$O + O_2 + M \longrightarrow O_3 + M \quad (11.14)$$

This stable ozone molecule reacts with nitric oxide to form nitrogen dioxide and an oxygen molecule.

$$O_3 + NO \longrightarrow NO_2 + O_2 \quad (11.15)$$

If ozone ions is present in excess, it reacts with nitrogen dioxide to form nitrogen pentoxide and oxygen.

$$2NO_2 + O_3 \longrightarrow N_2O_5 + O_2 \quad (11.16)$$

In the presence of atmospheric moisture, nitrogen pentoxide is formed to nitric acid

$$N_2O_5 + H_2O \longrightarrow 2HNO_3 \quad (11.17)$$

11.4.5 Sulphuric Acid Rain Formation

Sulphurdioxide molecule absorbs solar radiation and becomes highly energized molecule, which reacts with oxygen molecule to form sulphate ion.

$$SO_2 + h\nu \text{ (solar radiation)} \longrightarrow SO_2 \text{ (energized)} \quad (11.18)$$

$$SO_2 \text{ (energized)} + O_2 \longrightarrow SO_4 \quad (11.19)$$

This sulphate ion further reacts with molecular oxygen to form sulphite ion and ozone. In the presence of atmospheric moisture, sulphite ion undergoes to sulphuric acid.

$$SO_4 + O_2 \longrightarrow SO_3 + O_3 \quad (11.20)$$

$$SO_3 + H_2O \longrightarrow H_2SO_4 \quad (11.21)$$

This process is carried with low efficiency.

11.4.6 Programs

Earth Summit: An international conference on sustainable development, popularly known as " Earth Summit" (United Nations Conference on Environment and Development) held on 3rd to 14th June 1992 at Rio De Janeiro (Brazil). The conference was intended to high light the global problems for sustainable development. 178 nations participated in this conference to prepare a comprehensive document that will set the planet Earth on a new course of stainable development and save the fragile earth from environmental degradation. The agenda is intended to provide a blue print of action in all areas relating to the sustainable development of the planet until the 21st centuary. The Agenda 21 covered on genuine commitment to the ethic of care and goal of sustainability in global environmental problems like green house effect, depletion of ozone layer and acid rain etc.

The United Nations has estimated that \$125 billions is needed annually to implement Agenda 21, which is the conference blue print for cleaning the planet Earth. At least \$10 billions is required to start in initial year. But richest countries (Japan, Germany, Great Britain, U.S.A., France etc.) offer was only \$2 billions.

References

Bethea, R.M. "Air Pollution Control Technology" Van Nostraand Reinhold Company, New York, 1978.

Bibbero, R.J. and Young, I.G. "systems approach to air pollution control" John Wiley & Sons, New York, 1974.

Bureau of Indian Standards 'Codes of air pollution' IS: Manak Bhavan, 9, Bahadur Shah Zafar Marg, New Delhi-2.

Chanlett, ·E.T. "Environmental Protection" McGraw-Hill Company Limited, New York 1974.

Crawford Martin "Air Pollution Control Theory" Tata McGraw-Hill Publishing Company Limited, New Delhi, 1980.

Liptak, B.G. 'Environmental Engineer's Hand Book' Vol. 2, Air Pollution, Chilton Book Company, Pennsylvania, 1974.

Lyons, T.J. and Scott, W.D. 'Principles of Air Pollution Meteorology' Belhaven Press, London, 1990.

Masters, G.M. 'Introduction to Environmental Engineering and Science, Prentice-Hall of India Private Limited, New Delhi, 110001, 1991.

NEERI, Air quality in selected cities in India, Report, 1981.

Painter, D.E. "Air Pollution Technology" Prentice-Hall Company, Virginia, 22090, 1974.

Peavy, H.S. "Environmental Engineering", McGraw-Hill Co., New York, 1985.

Perkins, H.C. "Air Pollution" McGraw-Hill, Kogakusha Limited, Tokyo, 1974.

Rao, C.S. "Environmental Pollution Control Engineering", Wiley Eastern Limited, New Delhi, 1991.

Rao, M.N. and Rao, H.V.N. "Air Pollution" Tata McGraw-Hill Publishing Company Limited, New Delhi, 1989.

Seinfeld, J.A. 'Air Pollution' Mcgraw-Hill Book Company, New York, 1975.

Shivaji Rao, T. "Elements of Air pollution and its control" published by Mrs. T. Lavanya Lata, Visakhapatnam -3, 1988.

Strausss, W.'Air Pollution' Wiley-Interscience, New York, 1971.

Stern, A.C. 'Air pollution', Vol. 1, third edn., Academic Press, New York, 1976.

Thedore, and Huonicore "Industrial Air Pollution Contol" equipment for particulates, CRC Press, 1975.

Turk, A., Turk, J., Wittes, J.T., and Writters, R. "Environmental Science", 2nd edn., W.B. Saunders Company, Philadelphia. 1974.

Turner, D.B. "Workbook on atmospheric dispersion estimates" P.H.S. Publication. 999-AP-26, 1970.

Wark, Kenneth and Warner, C.F. "Air Pollution" 2nd edn., Harper and Row Publishers, New York, 1981.

WHO "Air Pollution" Columbia University Press, New York, 1961.

APPENDICES

APPENDIX I

Conversion Factors: ppm to μg/m³

A. (At 25 °C and 760 mm Hg)

Parameter	Molecular Weight	ppm	μg/m³	At 0 °C 760 mm Hg μg/m³
SO_2	64	1	2620	2860
CO	28	1	1145	1250
NO_2	46	1	1881	
NO	30	1	1227	
NH_3	17	1	695	
O_3	48	1	1963	2141
PAN[$CH_3(CO)O_2NO_2$]		1	4945	5398

B. $$\mu g/m^3 = \frac{(ppm) \times \text{Molecular weight}}{24{,}450} \times 10^6$$

$$ppm = \frac{(\mu g/m^3) \times 24{,}450}{\text{Molecular Weight} \times 10^6}$$

C. 1% Volume/Volume = 10,000 ppm

Note: Conversion factors at 0 C and 760 mm use 22400 instead of 24450 in B.

APPENDIX II

List of Indian Standards Relating to Air Pollution

Glossary of terms relating to air pollution		4167–1966
Methods for measuring air pollution :		
Part I	Dustfall	5182 (Part I)-1969
Part II	Sulphur dioxide	5182 (Part II)-1969
Part III	Radioactivity (particulate) in air	5182 (Part III)-1970
Part IV	Suspended matter	5182 (Part IV)-1973
Part V	Sampling of gaseous pollutants	5182 (Part V)-1975
Part VI	Nitrogen oxides	5182 (Part VI)-1973
Part VII	Hydrogen sulphide	5182 (Part VII)-1973
Part VIII	Sulphation rate	5182 (Part VIII)-1976
Part IX	Oxidants	5182 (Part IX)-1974
Part X	Carbon monoxide	5182 (Part X)-1976
Part XI	Benzene	5182 (Part XI)-1982
Part XII	Polynuclear aromatic hydrocarbons in air particulate matter	5182 (Part XII)-1974
Part XIV	Guidelines for planning the sampling of atmosphere	5182 (Part XIV)-1979
Part XV	Mass concentration of particulate matter in the atmosphere	5182 (Part XV)-1974
Part XVI	Recommended practice for collection by filtration and determination of mass, number, and optical sizing of atmosphere particulates	5182 (Part XVI)-1980
Part XVII	C_1 and C_5 hydrocarbons in the air by gas chromatography	5182 (Part XVII)-1979

Part XVIII Continuous analysis and automatic recording of the oxidant content of the atmosphere	5182 (Part XVIII)-1974
Part XIX Chlorine	5182 (Part XIX)-1982
Part XX Carbon disulphide	5182 (Part XX)-1982
Micrometeorological techniques in air pollution studies, guidelines for	8829-1978
Nitric acid and nitrogenous fertiliser industries, limits for gaseous emissions from	9005-1978
Ringlemann and miniature smoke charts, code for use of	9078 - 1979
Smoke emission levels for diesel vehicles	8118 - 1976
Vehicles powered by spark ignition engines, emission limits for carbon monoxide	9057 - 1986
Gaseous emissions from man-made fibre plants, limits for:	
Part I Cellulosic fibres	9233 (Part-I) - 1979
Guide for units used in Air Quality Measurements	9260 - 1980
Code for practice for Work Environment Monitoring (airborne contaminants)	9679 - 1980
Control of air pollution in petroleum refineries	10,179 - 1982

APPENDIX III

Reagents Preparation for Analysis of Air Pollutants

1. Reagents preparation for estimation of sulphur dioxide in air:

Absorbing solution: 0.1 M Sodium tetrachloromecurate : Dissolve 27.2 g (0.1 mole) mercuric chloride and 11.7 g (0.2 mole) sodium chloride in one litre of distilled water.

ρ-Rosaniline Hydrochloride:

Dissolve 0.2 g in 100 ml of distilled water and filter the solution after 48 hours.

Sodium sulphite solution : Dissolve 640 mg of sodium metabisulphite in 1 litre of water and standardized by titration with standard 0.01 N iodine with starch as indicator.

Formaldehyde solution: Dilute 5 ml of 40% formaldehyde solution to 1 litre with distilled water.

2. Reagents preparation for estimation of oxides of nitrogen in air :

Absorbing reagent: Dissolve 4 g of sodium hydroxide in distilled water and dilute in1000 ml.

Sulphanilamide: Dissolve 20 g of sulphanilamide in 700 ml of distilled water. Add, with mixing, 50 ml of concentrated phosphoric acid and dilute to 1000 ml.

NEDA solution: Dissolve 0.5 g of N (1-naphthyl) ethylenediamine dihydrochloride in distilled water.

Hydrogen peroxide: Dilute 0.2 ml of 30% of hydrogen peroxide to 250 ml with distilled water.

3. Reagent preparation for estimation of hydrogen sulphide in air :
Absorbing solution: Dissolve 4.3 g of cadmium sulphate in water. Add 0.3 g of sodium hydroxide dissolved in a small amount of water and dilute to one litre and mix well.

4. Reagents preparation for estimation of oxidants in air :
Absorbent : Dissolve 14 g of potassium dihydrogen phosphate, 14.2g of disodium hydrogen phosphate and 10 g of potassium iodide successively and dilute to mixture to one litre with distilled water.
Standard Iodine solution : Dissolve 16 g of potassium iodide and 3.17 g of iodine successively and dilute the mixture with distilled water to exactly 500 ml to make a 0.05 N solution.

5. Reagents preparation for estimation of fluorides in air:
SPADNS solution: Dissolve 0.985 g of SPADNS dye in water and dilute to 500 ml.
Zirconium solution : Dissolve 0.265 g of zirconyl chloride octahydrate in 50 ml of water, add 700 ml of concentrated hydrochloric acid and dilute to 1:1 with water.
(Reproduced with kind permission from Bureau of Indian Standards)